Additional Praise for *A Cup of Water Under My Bed*

Featured on *Kirkus Reviews*' Best of 2014 Nonfiction List

"Hernández's story is not just about a young woman trying to find herself; it's also about those invisible immigrant women, like her mom and aunts, who have been relegated to the background. Hernández dares to tell their stories too."

—Bust Magazine

"*A Cup of Water Under My Bed* is a wonderful, heartbreaking, necessary story for all women and men, but foremost for other women of color. I wish this book had been available for me when I was making my foolish way in my perilous twenties, but how glorious that it's available now. During a time in history when so much is said about women of color, working-class folks, immigrants, Latinas, poor people, and *los despreciados*, but seldom from them, Hernández writes with honesty, intelligence, tenderness, and love. I bow deeply in admiration and gratitude."

– Sandra Cisneros,
author of *The House on Mango Street*

"Reading the book is like looking at a life through a piece of holey lace crocheted by your *tia*."

—Feministing

"Written in the tradition of great feminist memoirs, like Audre Lorde's *Zami* and Minnie Bruce Pratt's *S/HE*, while nodding, particularly in the first section, to Sandra Cisneros's extraordinary *House on Mango Street*, Hernández's *A Cup of Water Under My Bed* explores race, gender, and sexuality with beauty and grace."

—Lambda Literary

"Journalist, feminist, and first-time memoirist Hernández presents a coming-of-age story that dives into the complexities of language, sexuality, and class. . . . An accessible, honest look at the often heart-wrenching effects of intergenerational tension on family ties."

—Booklist

"This heartbreaking, wish-I-had-this-when-I-was-growing-up debut mixes prose you can taste with memoir, narrative, and social criticism in a way that's necessary and reflective of real life."

—*Guernica*

"*A Cup of Water Under My Bed* is a courageous and compassionate exploration of one woman's journey from her roots to her truest self, and a wise and tender portrait of the women who shaped her existence. . . . A striking and illuminating memoir of stark beauty that challenges our notions of identity and feminine power; absolutely riveting and unforgettable."

—Patricia Engel,
author of *It's Not Love, It's Just Paris*

"This book is a compelling glimpse into the life of a young Latina struggling to hold onto her background and make her way in a world she often finds difficult to embrace. Hernández's use of language is often poetic, especially when intermingling Spanish and English, with the cultural tones of each."

—*The Windy City Times*

"With wit and respectful grace, Hernández shares stories of love for family, of strong (despite herself) roots, and of assimilation and claiming who you are without losing who you were."

—*Dallas Voice*

"*A Cup of Water Under My Bed* is easily one of the most engaging memoirs I've read in years. Hernández is a stone-cold truth teller, and her talent is eclipsed only by her fearlessness. If this debut is a sign of what's to come, plan to have your heart and head broken wide open. Again and again."

—John Murillo,
author of *Up Jump the Boogie*

A Cup of Water Under My Bed

A Cup of Water
Under My Bed
a memoir

Daisy Hernández

Beacon Press
Boston

Beacon Press
Boston, Massachusetts
www.beacon.org

Beacon Press books
are published under the auspices of
the Unitarian Universalist Association of Congregations.

23 22 21   13 12 11

This book is printed on acid-free paper that meets the uncoated paper
ANSI/NISO specifications for permanence as revised in 1992.

Text design and composition by Kim Arney

Some chapters in this book were previously published in slightly different
versions in *Fourth Genre; Bellingham Review; Hunger Mountain: the VCFA Journal
of the Arts; Wise Latina: Writers on Higher Education* (University of Nebraska
Press, 2013); *Border-Line Personalities: A New Generation of Latinas Dish on Sex,
Sass and Cultural-Shifting* (Harper Paperbacks, 2004); and *Without a Net: The
Female Experience of Growing Up Working Class* (Seal Press, 2004).

Library of Congress Cataloging-in-Publication Data
Hernández, Daisy.
A cup of water under my bed : a memoir / by Daisy Hernandez.
pages   cm
ISBN 978-0-8070-6292-0 (paperback : alkaline paper)
ISBN 978-0-8070-1449-3 (ebook)
1. Hernández, Daisy. 2. Hernández, Daisy—Family. 3. Young women—Family
relationships—United States. 4. Colombian Americans—Biography. 5. Cuban
Americans—Biography. 6. Bisexual women—United States—Biography.
7. Identity (Psychology)—United States. 8. Women—New Jersey—Biography.
9. Women journalists—New York (State)—New York—Biography.
10. United States—Social conditions—1980– I. Title.
CT275.H5862453A3 2014
920.009268'7291073—dc23
2014000820

para todas las hijas

"What does a woman inherit
that tells her how
to go?"

—Sandra Cisneros

Contents

Condemned

A town official came to our home one day. It was a kind of inspection since my father was itching in those years to build an addition to the original house, and he needed certain permits. When the white man arrived, he had a clipboard in his left hand and began examining windows and fire alarms, then frowning and scribbling notes.

Our house sat in a small corner of northern New Jersey, and it was a very old house. It had no basement, no closets, no doors on the bedrooms. The living room was a box of a place and the kitchen took up most of the first floor.

Standing there in our kitchen, the town official muttered, "This house should be condemned."

My mother wanted to know what he had said. *"Qué dijo?"*

"Nada."

I don't remember now if I actually said, "Nothing," or if I stayed silent. I was about twelve at the time and I didn't know the Spanish word for condemned. I didn't have a word in our language that would say, This photograph on the wall, this pot of black beans, this radio we listen to each day, these stories you tell us—he's saying none of this matters. It should not only be thrown away but bulldozed.

I began writing this memoir in 2000 when the feminist magazine *Ms.* gave me a regular column in its pages. I was twenty-five and terrified to write for real people who might condemn me, so I wrote about what I thought I knew, like why my mother didn't call herself a feminist and why we wanted advice from women who talked to dead people.

When my contract with *Ms.* ended, I continued writing. I wanted to understand my mother's questions and my auntie who thought I was *una india* and my father who drank too much. I needed to see on paper the women and the father I had loved and resisted and betrayed, and to write them without the *mancha* of a white man who thought our lives and our stories should be bulldozed.

I wanted, too, to testify. To say: This happened. These quiet stories were taking place when the suits in Washington were waging their private wars in Central America, when they began shoving the border into the desert, when they insisted, "Don't ask, don't tell," when they signed NAFTA and everyone began seeking the safety of corners. My mother and father prayed harder. My auntie told another *cuento.* I wrote it all down. To believe that my story, our story, any story stood by itself was dangerous. Feminists taught me this. Journalism confirmed it.

Journalism: A fancy word to say that I spent days with my hands in other people's stories, asking and telling, because nothing happens in isolation, especially when it has to do with language. Nothing is more vulnerable than the words in our mouths, because nothing has more power.

I had words in 1980. They were the color of copper and ash and pomegranates.

But Ronald Reagan was elected president that year and John Lennon was shot, and before that, it was morning and they had come for me.

one

Before Love, Memory

They come for me in a station wagon. My mother already has me dressed in a navy-blue plaid jumper and a white blouse. She has yanked my dark hair into pigtails and now makes the sign of the cross on my forehead before turning me over to a skinny lady, who ushers me into the backseat of the station wagon. I join a small group of children, mostly Cuban, all of us dressed alike, our eyes bright and nervous.

The station wagon lady drops us off at the steps of a gloomy castle in Union City, New Jersey: Holy Family Catholic School. The yard is hemmed in with black iron bars and the front doors are made of steel. Women in dress pants roam the cement grounds like fat hens with their wings clipped, their beaks pointing and gesturing. I huddle with the other children in packs of three and five like scared chicks.

Miss Reynolds is the kindergarten teacher. She has glasses that make her eyes look like oversized buttons on her face, and she speaks the funny language that comes out of the television set at home when we are not watching telenovelas or the *noticias*, which is to say that she talks like the cartoon character Mighty Mouse. It is English, a language that sounds like marbles in the mouth. It is fun to hear, but mostly because the mouse on the TV screen is flying.

Sitting in the classroom, I wait for Miss Reynolds to start talking like my mother. In Spanish. Surely it won't be long now. An hour passes. Two hours. An entire day it feels, and still it is all Mighty Mouse.

I am familiar with the language. I even speak a few words of it. But I have never heard so much of it all at once. It's like being forced to watch the same cartoon all day long.

I don't know if this is what actually happened on my first day of kindergarten, but it is what I remember of my first two years in school. A few memories can be confirmed by research and on-site inspection: Mighty Mouse on television, the school's black iron bars. My mother verifies the station wagon lady and the ethnicity of the other children, and school photographs offer details of the uniform and my teacher's face.

There are, however, missteps in memory, places where emotion has distorted people, sights, even *cuerpos*. In a school photograph, for example, my teacher is a skinny, androgynous white woman with thick glasses. But I remember her as a fat hen, a flying mouse, and kindergarten as the beginning of the end.

A teacher comes for us one day. Just two of us. Me and my friend, a thin, pixie-faced girl.

I don't know why we are being taken from class, but in the darkened hallway as we find ourselves farther from our classroom, my friend starts crying, and hers are not baby tears. They are full blast, *llorona* wails. She roots herself to the ground and refuses to take one more step. The teacher begins dragging her by the arm, but the harder the woman pulls, the more my friend yells and twists, and for an instant, it looks as if her left arm is threatening to rip from her body, as if she will choose self-mutilation over what is to come at the hands of white women. As for myself, I don't fight. I follow.

In an empty classroom, the white woman pulls out a deck of cards with pictures and words. She spreads the cards on a broad table, one by one. The sun is pouring through the window and coating us in a yellow liquid, but I can decipher the cards. Each one holds a picture and a word: *dog, cat, house.* I am to repeat each word after the teacher.

In Spanish, we have *cartas.* Tía Rosa's husband uses them to talk with the spirit world. The cards tell us about jobs that are about to arrive, ancestors who are unhappy, a case pending with immigration. The cards are paper doors only special people can open.

I look at the white woman's cards and listen to her bold English words—*dog, cat, house*—and there is all the evidence of what is to come in my life. I am not to go the way of the two people I long for in the thick terror of the night. The first man I love and the first woman I adore, my father and my mother with their Spanish words, are not in these cards. The road before me is English and the next part too awful to ask aloud or even silently: What is so wrong with my parents that I am not to mimic their hands, their needs, not even their words?

Before language, there is love. Before love, memory.

What I know of the world before kindergarten is the uneven sidewalks of Union City, New Jersey. The shop with its fat chickens hollering at us and nipping at the wire cages. The sharp smell of chicken blood when the little beasts are killed in back and brought in white plastic bags to my mother. The fabric store with its bins carrying spools of thread like a Cubana holding up the ends of her apron. The buses that snake up and down Bergenline Avenue. The store jammed with cigars and wrinkled men and women folding the ends of the thick brown leaves.

Our national language is Spanish and there are many kinds. Mostly it is the firecracker Spanish of my Cuban father and his friends. It smacks the air and the back of my head and the inside of my ears. There is also the Spanish of the Puertorriqueño Tía Rosa has married. His words mimic popcorn when it first begins popping. Finally, there is Colombian Spanish. My mother's language does not crack or bounce. It stays close to the earth, to thick hands and the smooth sides of stones.

English has a place here. It is the language of minorities, and you hear it every now and then, mostly from Mighty Mouse on television or the older kids on the block. English is a game of marbles. The words shoot after each other. They bump and plod and leave tracks on the ground, and it is a decent game, English that is, but everything real happens in Spanish: the way women complain about the *fábricas* where they work, how they yell at you to not play in the street, how they drag you into the house when the sky turns a velvet black, lying to you: "*Ahorita sales otra vez.*"

Terrible things happen in Spanish.

My father and his friend get drunk, slur their words, and turn into screeching birds. Rage is an awful habit in any language, I suppose, but on our street, in our home, in Spanish, it takes on awful proportions, and the mothers complain to each other in shorthand: "*Qué se va 'cer?*" The reply is always the same: *Así son los hombres.*

Women are different.

Union City is filled with virgins. La Caridad, La Altagracia, La Virgen de Chiquinquirá. They come from Cuba, the Dominican Republic, and Colombia. Like us, they are a matter of multiplicity. There is never one of anything in this world. There are many virgins, many women, many sounds in Spanish.

Dollars, though, are a constant. In the kitchen, my mother folds aluminum foil over dollar bills and packs them into envelopes. The dollars are to be mailed with letters to her mother in Colombia.

We send dollars because of the wars. It is the eighties and there are two wars. The one in Colombia is about land and poor people. The other one, the Cold War, means my mother and I cannot travel to Cuba. "It isn't safe," my father says in between puffs of his thick cigar.

We travel instead to Hialeah, Florida, and Mami and I go together by plane to Bogotá and Boyacá, and by train to Queens and Manhattan. By the time I start kindergarten, I feel these places and New Jersey are part of the same country. Everyone lives within its borders, speaks Spanish, and eats a lot of fried pork.

In the evening, my mother turns on the television for the *noticias*. The stories arrive from Latin America. Women with missing teeth cry into microphones. Men with brown faces scream. *Los niños* carry younger children. Sometimes, it is only the image of men's feet in their shoes and the white sheets covering the rest of their bodies. The women wail behind the reporter, who talks about the number of dead and those left behind.

"*Ay, los pobres*," my mother whispers, before turning her eyes and her pregnant belly away from the television screen.

But I don't look away. I want to see what it is all about, because my mother comes from that place in the television set and so does my father. Those places where the floor is a thick brown soil and men's bodies disappear save for their shoes.

At Holy Family, report cards are made of heavy stock paper and folded once with your name handwritten on the cover. Inside, Miss Reynolds has seared the letters *U* and *I* across the squares, because, according to her, I am unsatisfactory or need improvement in starting work promptly, reading books, accepting responsibility, speaking English, and, yes, even singing.

Nine months later, every line of my report card is filled with the letter *S*, the curves leaning into my new future. Satisfactory. The only category that eludes me is the "oral expression of ideas." The ability to speak English. There Miss Reynolds has written a tilting but nevertheless insistent *I*. Improvement needed.

My mother searches for the only English words she knows on the report card: parent signature, and there in her best penmanship learned in Colombia, she signs her name: Alicia Hernández.

We are both proud of her signature. The poverty in Latin America means that many people do not know how to sign their names, let alone read or write. Penning your name is a sign of progress, no matter what you are signing.

My mother makes recordings on cassette tapes to ship to her sisters and mother back home. She documents local gossip, my father's business ventures, and me at the age of four recounting the story of Little Red Riding Hood in Spanish. She insists I say something in English. Anything. But I am four. All I know are a few numbers. She says that's fine.

I begin: "One, two, three, four . . ." I pause, turn to my mother. "*Y después qué va?*"

Her voice, an accented English that so many years later strikes me as the voice of a stranger, replies, "Five," and I repeat the word. She says, "Six," and I repeat it, my voice dancing after hers, until we reach the number twenty.

Numbers are important in our lives. There are the two black garbage bags filled with fabric that a man brings to our apartment every few days. The dozens of women's pants my mother can produce on her Merrow sewing machine. The hundred dollars she is paid when the man comes for the bags at the end of the week.

Numbers are why my mother came to New Jersey, why she spent nights crying, wishing she could go back to Colombia, to her mother.

The author Minal Hajratwala has written, "Perhaps only we of the next generation—raised among strangers, eating the fruits of our parents' risks—can taste the true proportions of bitter to sweet."

By the end of kindergarten, my mouth is full of fruit, and as each year arrives, I stuff myself with more English words. I memo-

rize nursery rhymes and numbers, and I sit on my bed with vocabulary books, committing to memory nouns, adjectives, and
adverbs, while in the kitchen, my mother hollers, "*Llegó Walter!*"

Walter Mercado arrives on the television screen. He has
blond hair that has been set with hairspray into the 1980s look of
being eternally windswept. Thick layers of foundation coat his
pale face, and a deep coral lipstick shapes his lips. He sports elegant suits and over his shoulders capes studded with glittery *piedras*
that look like rhinestones, diamonds, and emeralds. Each cape is
said to be worth ten thousand dollars.

But Walter is like us. He speaks Spanish. He looks directly into
the television camera and into our hearts, lifts his right hand, and,
quickly and authoritatively, proclaims our daily horoscope. We
can expect a gift. We can expect the doors to open. We can expect
good health.

Walter Mercado is normal. White women are a different story.

We move, as Mami would say, *al Norte*.

In 1982, this means about five miles north of Union City and
four miles from the George Washington Bridge. I am seven years
old, and Papi has found the two-story house with no basement or
closets. Our own home, and in the front yard, a tree. A few blocks
away is the factory where he works nights. A block away is my new
school. Into the large shed in the yard, Mami squeezes her two
sewing machines and plastic bags of *telas* and extra bobbins and
scissors and fat spools of thread.

Fairview is a quiet town, a white town, an English-only town.
The neighbors bring us tomatoes. "They think we're Italian," my
mother giggles, as if she has snuck a puppy into her parents' house.

In Fairview, white women teach at my school and shop at a
place called Macy's. They go to Florida in the winter, even though
they have no cousins there. They have aunties who do not live
with them, and they are not like the white kids in my class whose

grandmothers speak Italian and walk them to school in the mornings. The white women's grandmothers are dead. When they mention Poland, Ireland, or Germany, it sounds like they are talking about a sock they lost in the laundry. They are white now. American. They have no history, no songs, no past.

But they do have power.

They have the sharpness of chalk, the sting of chemical cleaners for the blackboards, the clean earth smell of sharpened lead pencils. They have the respect of my parents. By virtue of their English and the light color of their faces, these teachers determine the words that creep into my dreams at night.

I envy them. I want what they have. I want my words to matter.

My mother's sisters come and go over the years, but finally they arrive, one by one, to stay. No more back and forth. They have no children and no husbands in Colombia. Their mother is dead. Their father, too. They are three pieces of thread cut from the spool.

Tía Dora. Tía Rosa. La Tía Chuchi.

The three were school teachers in Colombia. Tía Dora is the youngest, a piece of silk *hilo*. In Jersey, she scrubs toilets for a white lady down the shore and later gets a certificate to teach Spanish. Tía Rosa is the oldest, with hair like black cotton and *tacones* with thick heels. She cleans up after a white woman in the city. Tía Chuchi wears lush red lipstick to church every day and has stories better than the Bible's. Like my mother, she stitches sleeves to women's blouses at the factory. When the three aunties are home, they dote on my baby sister and work on me and my Spanish.

I call the carpet *la carpeta*, and Tía Dora shakes her head. She lifts her thin, fairy-like hands. "*Se dice alfombra,*" she says, and then slowly pronounces the word for me: *al-fom-bra. Carpeta* is the word for folder.

My mother tells me that my new friend has called. When I reply, *"La voy a llamar pa' tras,"* Tía Maria de Jesus, better known as La Tía Chuchi, puckers her bright lips. In Spanish, she lectures, "You never say, 'I am going to call you back.' *Eso es del inglés."* The verb, she declares, is *devolver. "Voy a devolver la llamada."*

If Tía Rosa is there, she comes to my defense, wrapping me up in her arms, the top of my head smashing into her large bosom. "Leave the girl alone," she says to her sisters, crooning like a bird at her nest. For a moment, I believe this auntie will call a cease-fire. But no, Tía Rosa thinks the war is over. "Stop bothering the girl. She's Americana." She pats the top of my head hard, as if I were mentally disabled.

My mother is different. She believes in truces, neutral zones, even treaties. Together, we stick the Spanish *el* or *la* before English nouns, producing words like *el* vacuum, *el* color purple, *la* teacher. We say, *"Abra la* window," *"Papi está en el* basement," *y "Ya pagamos el* mortgage." This is not easy. It takes time, negotiation, persistence.

In the morning, late for school, I call for my mother, alarmed. I can't find *mi* folder.

"Tu qué?"

"El folder," I answer, panicked. *"Donde pongo mis papeles pa' la escuela, Mami."*

"Ah, el folder," she says, quietly repeating the English noun to herself.

I begin resenting Spanish.

At first, it happens in small ways. I realize I can't tell my mother about the Pilgrims and Indians because I don't know the Spanish word for Pilgrims. I can't talk about my essay on school safety because I don't know the Spanish word for safety. To share my life in English with my family means I have to give a short definition for each word that is not already a part of our lives. I try sometimes, but most of the time I grow weary and finally sigh and mutter, *"Olvídate."* Forget it.

This is how Spanish starts annoying me.

I suppose it's what happens when you're young and frustrated, but you can't be angry at the white teachers because that would get you nowhere, and you can't be too upset with your parents because they want what they think is best for you. Spanish is *flaca* and defenseless, so I start pushing her around, then hating her. She's like an auntie who talks louder than everyone else, who wears perfume that squeezes your nostrils. I want her to stop embarrassing me. I want her to go away.

That's how the blame arrives. I blame Spanish for the fact that I don't know more words in English. I blame her for how bad I feel when the white teachers look at me with some pity in their eyes. I blame Spanish for the hours my mother has to work at the factory.

"If only I knew English . . ." my mother starts, and then her voice trails because none of us, not her, not even La Tía Chuchi, who knows everything about everyone, knows what would happen if only my mother knew English. I am the one who is supposed to find out.

But to make that leap, to be the first in a family to leave for another language hurts. It's not a broken arm kind of hurt. It's not abrupt like that. It's gradual. It is like a parasite, a bug crawling in your stomach that no one else can see but that gives you a fever and makes you nauseous.

Because I have to leave Spanish, I have to hate it. That makes the departure bearable. And so I never learn to read or to write the language. I never learn more than the words my family and I need to share over the course of a day—*pásame la toalla, la comida ya está*—and the words spoken on the nightly news, the telenovelas, Radio Wado, and *Sábado Gigante*, which all combined leave me with a peculiar vocabulary of words in Spanish about dinner foods, immigration law, romantic fantasy, and celebrity gossip.

As I become more immersed in English, I also start to distance myself from my family through unconscious gestures. I walk around the house with headphones on my ears and a book in hand. I speak only in English to my little sister. I eat my *arroz y frijoles* while watching the TV sitcoms *Diff'rent Strokes* and *Facts of Life*. The two shows—centered on children who don't have parents and are being raised by white people—make sense to me. I begin to convince myself that I am like my white teachers: I have no history, no past, no culture.

My father, however, still worries that I might become like him.

Sitting in the kitchen, slightly drunk, mostly sober, he grabs my arm. I am nine at the time, and he has my report card in his hand with the letter *F* in social studies.

"You have to study," he says, his brown eyes dull and sad. "You don't want to end up like your mother and me, working in factories, not getting paid on time. You don't want this life." His life. My mother and my tías' lives. And yet I do—though not the factories or the sneer of the white lady at the fabric store who thinks we should speak English. I want the Spanish and the fat cigars and Walter Mercado on TV every night. To love what we have, however, is to violate my family's wishes.

Years later, an Arab American writer smiles knowingly at me. "You betray your parents if you don't become like them," she tells me, "and you betray them if you do."

If white people do not get rid of you, it is because they intend to get all of you.

They will only keep you if they can have your mouth, your dreams, your intentions. In the military, they call this a winning hearts-and-minds campaign. In school, they call it ESL. English as a second language.

They come for me again in fourth grade. Me and a girl whose parents are from Yugoslavia. Down the hallway we trudge. In the room the table is the color of wet sand, and the teacher nods at us. She has books and consonants and vowels.

I memorize more words. I roll the marbles in my mouth and spit them out on tests and at English-only friends. I get a card to the town library and start checking out books by the dozens. I come to know the way the words in English hit each other on the page, and I begin reciting lines from *Romeo and Juliet*.

This affection for English happens the way some women talk about their marriages: you do it at the beginning because it's practical, because you need the green card, because all the jobs are here, but then the *viejo* grows on you. You come to know the way he likes his *café* or how he snores when he's having a bad dream. That is how it is for me with English. The affection comes later and settles in.

My mother warns me to not drown myself in a cup of water.

"*No te ahogues en un vaso de agua*" could be translated as "Don't sweat the small stuff," but because I am learning English from British novels and hours spent diagramming sentences, I don't know American idioms. I don't know how other children are counseled to not worry about a lost pen. I only know that, according to my mother, I shouldn't mistake a glass of tap water for the deep end of the swimming pool.

Quietly, over the years, I create literal translations in English for everything my family says in Spanish. *Échate la bendición*. Throw yourself into the blessing. *Dios le da carne al que no tiene muelas*. God gives meat to those who have no teeth. *Me ronca el mango*. The mango does something terrible to you.

When I consult my sister, Liliana, about a friend's dilemma, she shakes her head. "*No tienes velas en ese entierro*," she answers solemnly. You don't have candles at that funeral, and if you don't have candles at a funeral in Ramiriquí, Colombia, where my mother and her sisters were raised, it means the dead person is not your family. Everyone there knows the dead need four *velas* to light the corridors from this life to the next, and it is the responsibility of the dead person's family to bring those four candles and place them alongside the body. If the dead person is not your auntie or your *primo* or your own mother, then you should mind your business and not add your candles to someone else's funeral.

Words and *dichos* are like the spirits of the *muertos*. They belong to a specific time and place, but they move. They fly. They survive colonization and poverty. They adapt themselves to new geographies, flourish even.

When I tell my father that I am going to be a writer, he whistles and says, "*Ahora si que está tostada.*" Literally, this means I am toasted; it is the way Cubans say you've gone crazy.

White women dream for you.

In high school, my English teacher, Mrs. Spielvogel, fastens her large blue eyes on me. "If you go to Europe, go to Scotland," she says.

"Why?"

"It's magical. Everyone wants to go to England, but go to Scotland."

I nod, as if my family sits around watching *Sábado Gigante* and debating vacations to Europe, but in a way, Mrs. Spielvogel gives me the idea. Maybe I could go to Europe someday. Maybe I could even leave New Jersey.

My father doesn't know how *tostada* I am becoming by being in school all day, year after year, with white teachers. Or maybe he does.

In high school, I tape a picture of an electric typewriter to the refrigerator and he buys it for me. The exact model. An

IBM. He grins, watching me type my paper on Oscar Wilde, on the playwright's time in prison for being gay and this line from a poem of his which I don't understand but somehow makes sense to me: "Each man kills the thing he loves."

My father observes me for a few seconds bending over the electronic typewriter, then retreats to the kitchen for a can of Budweiser.

I enter the book publishing industry after college in the late nineties. I open mail for book editors, write rejection letters, and proofread flap copy. I spend day after day immersed in manuscripts, and at the end of every two weeks, I am paid on time. My mother beams. "And they pay *vacaciones*?" she asks. "And sick time, too?" Yes and yes.

She is happy for me, and I am expecting to feel the same. This job, after all, isn't just a job. It is the whole point of having learned English. This job is the reason Rosa Parks sat down and Dolores Huerta stood up and why my parents migrated here: so that people like me could work in places like this. It is a given that any moment now, I will feel a gush of joy and accomplishment that will be at once personal, communal, and historical. I imagine it will be like when Ed McMahon shows up at people's homes with a billboard-size check from American Family Publishing and the white woman or the black woman starts screaming and crying and hitting her husband on the shoulder.

I expect it to feel that good.

Instead, I find myself one day in the conference room, listening to a presentation about upcoming books. It's late in the afternoon already and they are debating what will make one book sell better than others on the market. I'm sitting by the window, and soon the room begins to feel too warm. The sunlight is filtering in through the blinds, making me squint. I close my eyes for a second, and when I open them, the whole scene before me has shifted, has come into a different focus.

The white people look whiter than before. Their English sounds sharper. I feel dark, small, and confused, and I begin to suspect, perhaps for the first time, that happiness is not going to come from this place or from English.

This is the point in the story where you try to make things right, where you think you can still be the hero, where you believe, however naively, that the solution is to fix the past.

I register for a Spanish class at the Instituto Cervantes in Manhattan. There are about six students in a course designed for people who grew up speaking Spanish but didn't formally study the language. The teacher is a tall Española with thin legs and an interest in bilingual education. She gives us a topic and lets us talk freely for twenty minutes. We begin chatting and debating in Spanish as if we were in our mothers' kitchens, the *platanos* frying on the stove, *Primer Impacto* on TV.

Finally, *la profesora* interrupts us. That was good, she says kindly, and I almost believe her until she writes on the board all the Spanglish words we used and a string of verbs we didn't conjugate properly. Our syntax is English; our Spanish words those of a five-year-old.

For the pop quiz, she gives us a paragraph in Spanish. Make any corrections you see necessary. I start reading, my pen ready, but I don't pause when I reach the line that someone's going to "*parquear el carro.*" Of course, they're *parqueando*; how else would you say you're parking a car?

"*Estacionar,*" *la profesora* tells us.

The other students and I glance at each other nervously and try saying the new word aloud. We're going to *estacionar* the car. The word sounds strange, because all the words I hear in Spanish have *primos* in English. It is impossible to hear a word in one language without a reference to the other, and so "*estacionar* the Honda" sounds like I'm trying to park the car at Grand Central Station.

—⟋⟋⟋—

I begin reading in Spanish for the first time, and seeing in writing words I have only known in the mouths of the women who raised me.

champú, ardilla, toalla

cepillo, colerete, blusa

desbaratar, huecos, lunar

Because Spanish has been only an oral language for me, it is a peculiar sensation to read it. It's like meeting an auntie at JFK who has just arrived from Colombia. She hasn't seen you since you were a toddler, but she hugs you as if the two of you were intimate, *de confianza*. And you are. You are strangers who have a shared history. People say you look alike. *Tienen la misma cara.* The tía inspects you with a grin, pinching your cheeks, like you once really did know each other.

That's how it feels to read Spanish now. It is to be in the embrace of someone who loves you and who is also something of a stranger.

Twenty years after kindergarten, I return to Holy Family Catholic School. The building is not as gray or as large as I remember it, but the fear is still there in my throat as I march up to the school door. I try to shake it off and focus. I am a student journalist reporting on the growing Mexican community in Union City, and I need to act professional.

At the front door, a brown woman peers down at me: La Virgen de Guadalupe. The school has been closed and is now El Centro de Guadalupe. An image of the Mexican virgin is taped to the door with an announcement about an event. Her hands, *como siempre*, are clasped in prayer.

I stand at the door, speechless. The place where I began to learn English, to become white, has itself grown brown, Spanish, indigenous. I know this has to do with patterns of white flight, of migration, of global politics, but for that moment, I am five years old again and back home. There is no *one* of anything. There are many languages, many kinds of Spanish and English, of brown women and borders that do not shift beneath our feet but simply grow with every step we take.

Notebook in hand, I knock on the door.

Stories She Tells Us

My mother tells the same stories every night.

In her queen-size bed, I am lying on one side of her and my younger sister on the other. I am about six at the time. It's evening. My father is at the factory and the bedroom is silent. The windows are shut, the curtains drawn, and the edge of the tall dresser has vanished in the dark. I feel the weight of my mother's body next to mine. She's a *muñeca de trapo*, my mother, a large rag doll, a careful gathering of cotton fabric and thread and something unnamed but substantial. She sighs now in bed and begins telling the story she told the night before.

In her stories, my mother is the heroine, the *inocente* who scares easily and whom everyone knows to be gentle and kind. She is not ambitious. In fact, she wants nothing more than to grow up and marry a good man with blond hair and blue eyes and have children who look like him. This is what she tells my sister and me when the lights are turned off. She rubs our backs and whispers stories into our dark hair.

Always, she begins the stories at the beginning, which is to say the first time she left her mother.

It is the sixties; the violence is in the jungles of Colombia and Mami is in the capital. She is sixteen. She has left school. She wears clean, sturdy shoes and a knee-length skirt. Her black hair is curled, her face plump. She has never been beyond the border of school or home, but now here she is. In a factory, a *fábrica*. She spends days marking the fronts of men's blazers with *tiza*, so the women on the sewing machines will know exactly where to stitch the pockets.

The only women she has known are like her mother, women who don't wear lipstick, who marry young, who birth a dozen children, and bow their heads at church on weekday mornings. But this factory in Bogotá teems with a different sort of woman, the kind who sneers about men, brags about her nights, flaunts her intimacies. Their voices puncture the air like threaded needles. The women even curse.

"I'd never heard anything like it before," my mother whispers to us in the dark.

The bedroom around us tilts, becomes an unlit stage. At the age of six, I stare at this stage and try to imagine a woman who knows bad words in Spanish.

The second time she leaves her mother, Mami has doubts.

It had felt innocent at first, akin to a new love. The invitation from a friend to visit New Jersey, her sister's encouragement and the money *también*. The promises of how easy it would be over there. She would earn real money, that's what everyone said, and in *dólares*, more than she could make at a factory in Bogotá. She is twenty-eight and unmarried. She has no reason to not go. *Y ademas*, the men over there have hair the color of the sun and eyes clear like the ocean at San Andrés.

Here, my heart squeezes in terror at the thought that someone could lie to my mother of all people, my beautiful rag doll mother.

She pauses in her story. My mother is an expert in the relationship between silence and language. She knows when and for how long to permit the stillness to step in and take its sovereign place. It drives me crazy. I lean my face into her arm and ask, "And then what happened?"

"They said so many things," she answers.

She is young in the story, my mother, and she has said she will go north. She will leave her mother for the United States but only for a month. She will set eyes on the country where mountains are made of steel and glass, and she will work to earn the money to pay back her sister and then some.

But now it is true what they say: the time of leaving is the time of reckoning.

It is December 8, 1970. It is a Tuesday morning in Bogotá, and my mother can't stop thinking about what the Jewish forelady at the factory told her. "I've been there," the woman said about the United States, her voice thick and ominous. "It's a cold place, a difficult place."

The words rise and fall in my mother's mind, squeeze perhaps at the tender places of her belly. She has never been far from her mother. She remembers the forelady's warnings but keeps mute. The ticket has been paid for. It cost her sister a lot of money. It is nothing that can be changed.

I imagine her picking up the suitcase and giving her bed a long look. Then seeing she has no place to hide her doubt, she swallows it whole and shuts the door.

"And then what happened?"

It is my sister asking or me. I can't tell because I am fighting to stay awake, to hear the story I know by heart, the stories I hear every night.

And then what happened?

I am too young to know that this is the nature of children's stories. There is always the heroine. There is always the terrible moment when the road splits, when a girl finds herself alone on the stage having to choose between school and the factory, between her mother and the cursing women, between Colombia and New Jersey.

And there is always the child listening as anxiously this time as the first time she heard the story. There is always the child learning the nature of fear, the promise of happy endings.

The stories my mother tells are crowded with monsters.

There are the factory women who curse, the woman who invites her to come to the States, the woman who uses her as a distraction while shoplifting. Sometimes the monster is Rosa, the sister who lent her the cash to leave Colombia.

In the States, Mami expected to find dollars plastered on sidewalks like wet leaves. "That's what they used to say," she whispers. "That it grew on trees."

But nothing is what it was supposed to be. The Friday before she arrives in Jersey City, socialists bomb an oil refinery in nearby Linden. The flames shoot more than a thousand feet into the air, a blinding protest for Angela Davis and Bobby Seale.

My mother finds work at a factory, *cosiendo* women's blouses on a Merrow sewing machine. Some days, she has the sleeves, the empty *brazos*, and she prods them under the pulsing needle, stitches them to the *blusa*. Other days, the blouse is nothing but two sheets of green fabric, and Mami's work is to attach the two at the shoulder, the thick thread birthing the shape.

Soon, she has another job, and a third. She is desperate to pay off the debt to her sister.

At twenty-eight, she lies in bed in New Jersey *solita*, and she cries and wonders, "What did I do?" She thinks about what her mother may be doing in that moment. She imagines them all there at the house together—her sisters, her brothers, her sisters-in-law, the nephews and nieces, the cousins and neighbors. All of them together *sin ella*.

I listen to her, my heart no longer an organ in the body but a pillow that can be grabbed and squeezed up close to the throat. My eyes are closed and the world is only my mother's large ragdoll arm soft against my cheek, her Spanish with its measured silences, and that horrible knowledge—that a girl may have to live without her mother—weighs on my chest like a stone, like death.

In my mother's stories, women are named after soft drinks.

La Coca-Cola lives in West New York. She has a lapdog she walks around the neighborhood. She knows everyone, and everyone knows her, which is why she's named after the popular soft drink. In the early seventies, La Coca-Cola understands immigration law, and women and men, and even marriage. She introduces my mother to Ygnacio, a skinny Cuban, who is so smitten that he buys a car to drive Mami around town.

When the Cuban proposes marriage on a park bench a few months later, my mother's answer is not the frenzy of "Yes, *te quiero*" or the cautiousness of "I need to think it over." It is the practical: *No tengo papeles*.

She isn't a citizen. She isn't a resident. On paper, she is not even a tourist anymore.

My mother loves to tell the story of how she took me to Canada. This is a happy *cuento* and so it is not a bedtime story. It is one that can be told in the light of day when the aunties and neighbors are crowded around us at the picnic table in the yard. She took her baby to Canada.

"That doesn't count!" I object.

The lawyer said it did.

In those years, the mid-seventies, the border at the north was not a solid mass, nothing made of granite but rather a door that swung open and allowed women like my mother to claim they had been living out of the country, so they could be sponsored by their American husbands, or in this case, a Cuban-turned-American on paper.

"You were in Canada," she croons. "*En la barriga.*"

My own stomach tightens. "What did they say?" I ask, nervous at the prospect of hearing a terrible story. How did they want her to prove that she was married, that it wasn't fake?

She tilts her chin into the air, defiant. "What could they say? I was pregnant. What more proof is there?" She smiles, satisfied.

I gape at my mother. She hates places where people wear uniforms or suits. Hospitals, embassies, even banks make her anxious.

It is hard to imagine a time when she was bold enough to show her swollen belly to white men, to government officials.

She insists, though, that it was the other way around, that crossing the border into Canada, I was the one who kicked in protest. I was the one who wanted to be heard, to be felt, to be taken into account.

My mother has one bedtime story that makes her smile.

In this story, she is seven or eight. She's not in Bogotá yet. She's still in Ramiriquí, a dot of a town a few hours outside of Colombia's capital. She is with her mother at morning Mass. Standing there in the pews, listening to the priest drone at the altar, my mother catches sight of a woman and her son. The woman is fine, perfectly acceptable, but the boy . . .

"What was wrong with the boy?" I whisper from my side of the bed. I am eight and alarmed, imagining a missing eye, a nose askew.

"He was . . ." My mother pauses, smiles fondly, as if it's a silly story. "He was *negrito*."

The boy was black.

My mother, then only a girl my age, turns her young pale face to her mami and in a hush, she asks: "How can that woman love her child? He's *feo*."

My grandmother smiles or scowls or shakes her head. That's not the important part. What counts is what she said next: "No matter how ugly, a child is always beautiful to his mother."

The words shock my mother. She stares at the boy some more. She's young, my mother, and she cannot imagine that it is true, that a mother's love demands nothing of its beloved, not even whiteness.

On the second floor of our home one evening, the white board stands on a tripod. It is magnetized, which makes the board into a sheet of paper that has come alive. I place upon that alabaster landscape the plastic magnets in the shape of letters: A, B, C, D, E. The letters are bursts of blue and red and orange, and to me, at the age of nine or ten, they are precious. They are not letters, not even *letras* that in Spanish sound so dignified—they are the tiny springs and steady hands that make the day possible. They are reliable. My mother, I have decided, needs to have them. In English. I believe they will rescue her from the horrors of this lifetime: the loneliness of her bedtime stories, my father's rages, the forelady at the factory who doesn't pay on time, the reception-ist at the dental office who knows we're there on charity and talks about us in third person.

I stand at the white board. My mother sits before me and the bright letters. "Repeat after me," I instruct in Spanish and then switch to English. "A, B, C . . ."

My mother grins. She is not the young woman of her stories now, not the one bracing herself for a new world of sounds and terrors. She is not even a rag doll. She is sturdier, rounder, more reliable and promising, like a new spool of thread. Her hair is the dark red of the sun at dusk, the result of coloring it with Clairol. Her pale face is tired and satisfied. She has spent the day steeped in fabric and thread and women's voices at the factory. Now she is here with me to learn English.

She repeats after me—A, B, C—but something grabs her at-tention: The sound of my sister's voice in the other room. The clock signaling the hour for the telenovela. "*Pon atención*," I de-mand, my jaw as tense as a white schoolteacher's.

My mother feigns a guilty face and tries again. But then some-thing bigger happens (something is always happening). The phone rings. My sister wants more orange-flavored soda. An aun-tie arrives. And my mother leaps away with that vicious promise of "*Seguimos más tarde*," as if learning English were a game that could be interrupted, paused, and resumed at leisure.

I am so young. I think language is all a woman needs.

—◊◊◊—

As a child, I don't know how to find myself in stories.

Sometimes I am in my mother's *cuentos* and I understand what it means to leave your *mami* since I am leaving mine every day while I stumble over English verbs. Other times, I see myself in my social studies textbook. I am the Statue of Liberty, welcoming my mother to the land of the free, of the saved.

The textbooks carry pictures of women and men arriving at Ellis Island. The women in the photographs appear stoic, with obligatory bleak faces and thick eyebrows, their lips as thin as my mother's, and the caption begins: "They came . . ."

What comes next varies.

They came looking, they came searching, they came hoping—the verbs always more lively and ambitious than the women in the pictures, whose faces speak another refrain: "What the hell are you looking at?"

It must have been around the time I was nine that the stories moved. I must have wanted to be in my own bed at night, and my mother did not object. Her stories stepped into other moments of our lives, into that hour in her bedroom on Sunday mornings between waking and boiling water *para el café*.

Here, the curtains are still drawn, but the light of the day filters in. The room is golden. The dresser squeezed into the corner. The Virgin Mary, confined to a spot above the bed, watches over us, and my mother remembers the time she first learned what it means to be a woman.

She was in the shower. It should have been a normal day, but her mother had not told her about the bleeding. Now here it is: the red river between her legs, her back throbbing, and later her brothers laughing and telling her about the prostitutes they know. "I was so naïve," she sighs.

—ᴍ—

My mother wrote for a time. She penned letters to her mother and posted them in the mail in Jersey, but they never reached Colombia. "They thought I was dead," she says, the wrinkles forming at the corners of her eyes and lips. She tells us again about those days: the crushing solitude, the debt she had to pay, the factories.

But I am grown now. I am writing this story, and I have questions that feel harsh in the morning light and also necessary. Why was it my mother and not her brothers or sisters who left Colombia? Which is to say, why am I writing and not my friends or my sister? Why her and me? Why are we willing to leave home?

"I got the invitation," my mother answers, as if she has never told me the story. "I knew this lady who had worked with me in Colombia and she said, 'If I ever get to the United States, I'll send for you.'"

"But that can't be it," I argue.

It cannot be as simple as getting an invitation. There has to already be the trace of something in a person, a certain boldness, at least a longing.

The room at New York University has two sofas and a dim light. It's been a year since I finished college in Jersey, and now I squeeze in between the women on the long sofa. Three Latina feminists have organized a writing workshop here. An introduction is made and a South Asian woman in her twenties begins to read her work.

The story is about a girl whose family home is burned down in an act of racial hatred. The girl's father is distraught and enraged; the girl is standing apart, watching the burning. She hated the house like she hated her father, who lorded over that home, over her girl life, over her mother.

It is the first time I have known someone my age writing about loving and hating where you come from, about the terrible things a father does and the awful things the world does to him, and the mother standing by in that bitter silence. Running clear through the story is the love the girl feels for her family, their home, and, also, the anguish.

For me, this has all been a very private matter, a story not even whispered at bedtime. But here is a dark-haired woman sitting right in front of me, having written it all down, and I can see for the first time that shame and memories need not oppress us. Naming carries its own brilliant power.

In the kitchen, the light of the early evening flickers through the partially opened curtains, and my mother does not have a story for us today, but I have one for her.

Feminism, I want her to know, is what will liberate her. She should organize with the other women at the factory to demand their back wages. This is what women have done before. I've read about it.

"What's that?" my mother asks.

I am annoyed to have my story interrupted. "What's what?"

"*Femenís.*"

Her Spanish squeezes the word as if it were not an elegant arrangement of sounds, a whole body of ideas and stories and political actions, but an avocado she's pinching at the *supermercado*.

I don't know the word in Spanish for feminist, so I write about not knowing. I write about the places between Spanish and English, between my mother's stories and my own. When I am done, the piece is published in *Ms.* magazine, and I translate it into Spanish for my mother.

Before sharing it with her, I check my spelling. I read it several times. It's a crude rendering of the English version because I have no grace in Spanish, no intimacy with the syntax, but it is the best I can do.

Days later, when I ask my mother what she thinks of the piece, she says, "*Me dió tristeza.*" Not "I hated it," "I was shocked," "I think you're crazy." But "*Me dío tristeza.*"

The English translation—"It made me sad"—is not the equivalent of the Spanish. When a woman says in Spanish that something has made her sad, it sounds like she has kissed her child good-bye and boarded an airplane *pa' el Norte*. The words in Spanish make you want to look away, which is what I do, and my mother and I don't speak again about what I wrote.

A few weeks after, though, she is sitting next to me at the kitchen table and asks, "What are you reading?"

"A book," I say without taking my eyes off the page.

"Who wrote it?"

I look up, startled. I have spent most of my days since I was nine years old reading books at the kitchen table. I am twenty-five. My mother has never asked me for the name of an author.

"It's this woman . . . Gloria Anzaldúa," I say slowly, suspicious about her sudden interest. "She's Chicana, like Mexican, but born here."

My mother sips her *manzanilla* tea. "What does she write about?"

I stare at her, slightly disoriented. Before I can think too much, I am racing, the Spanish words stumbling out of my mouth as I explain Gloria's ideas of the borderlands, of living "in between" as feminists, as Colombianas, as women who belong to more than one land and one culture. We are neither here nor there, I conclude, almost out of breath. *Ni aquí, ni alla.*

My mother nods. She lowers her eyes to the book's cover, then looks back at me, waiting for more, and the idea begins to bloom in me: my mother already knows this.

It is a story as old as time, that we always find what we needed was right at home.

But, therein is the riddle: a child has to leave to return. My mother had to. She says it often. She only appreciated her mother, only understood her mother, after she had left home.

I had to leave, too. It was me, not my mother, who needed English, who needed the stories and feminist theories. Without them, I might never have come back to her.

I tell my mother I am writing about her life and ask what she wants me to include.

"I like to travel," she answers, cheerfully. "I like gardens, flowers."

Her favorite place (the place she still thinks about) is London, because somehow despite the number of children with black hair, my mother's eyes saw only the ones with blond ringlets and blue eyes. "They were *cochinitos*," she laughs, "but I would have cleaned them up."

My mother tried to clean me up when I was born.

She and Tía Chuchi scrubbed my face and arms and chest with soapy water and cow's milk. "You were so dark," Tía remembers, as if the color of my skin had been an illness.

It is Christmas Eve and the palm trees are swaying in the blue-black night. My mother, my sister, my father, and I are at a cousin's house in South Florida. A pig is being roasted in a corner of the yard, its pink skin browning in the earth, and someone has turned up the volume on the speakers. The music winds around us and the women start to dance.

My mother, now in her late sixties, begins an old dance, one from Colombia, from when she was *joven* and beautiful, she says. Her left hand lifts the edge of a long imaginary skirt. Her right hand reaches into the air as if to call forth a lover or the stars. Her feet tip to the left and to the right and her body follows.

I look at her and think: Who the hell is this woman? And then I feel the thread between us break loose and my mother is a separate woman from me, one with her own life, a separate country, if you will. Her arm is reaching into the sky like an inverted exclamation point. Her right hand is not calling anyone to her but is instead announcing her.

The Candy Dish

 My father keeps a candy dish in the shed. On the floor.

When my mother refuses to grant me any more sweets in the kitchen, I make my way to the shed, or *el cuartico*, as we call it. It's a small room attached to the front of our house and it holds the boiler that heats our home, my mother's two industrial-size sewing machines, a shelf of plastic bags stuffed with fabric, and my father's machete and hammer.

The candy dish is hidden behind the boiler.

My mother scolds me if she catches me here. My father does as well. If he's drunk, he yells, curses, even shoves me out of the shed. None of this deters me.

At the age of eight, I squeeze myself around the boiler's round white body, careful to avoid the grease spots on the ground. The candy dish waits for me back there, a clay plate filled with M&Ms, Tootsie Rolls, and caramel candies. A gray rock with cowrie shells for eyes and a mouth sits on that throne of *dulces*, and next to the plate, a white ceramic cup has been filled with Cuban coffee.

I have been getting candy this way since I was a toddler and the clay dish was tucked under my parents' bed. Over the years, I've learned to distinguish the new *dulces* from the old ones by examining the wrappers for dust and tears. I don't know why my parents hide the plate like this, but it doesn't bother me. It doesn't even annoy me. I'm used to it.

What does upset me in the *cuartico* is the other plate.

It's made of clay also but filled with tiny iron toys: a shovel, machete, rake, and anvil. In theory, a collection of toys sounds appealing, but the iron pieces appear angry, and I always have the nagging suspicion that they are about to fling themselves at me. I've learned to take the candy, avoid the little machete, and run out of the shed.

There's nothing odd about any of this, because it has always been this way. In my house, grown people hide candies and toys, even roosters.

I walk into the kitchen one day as my mother stands barefoot on the kitchen counter. She's dressed in a white T-shirt and a violet skirt, and she's carefully placing a tin rooster with bells at his feet on top of the cupboard.

She climbs down with some effort but also a look of satisfaction on her face, like she's Moses returning from the mountain with the Ten Commandments. She sees me and asks a normal question, like if I want pizza for lunch. If I ask her about the rooster or the candy dish, she will have the same answer: "*Son cosas de tu papá.*"

From the top of the cupboard, the tin rooster's bells are silent, but I can feel him watching us, his eyes soft and gray.

In Catholic elementary school, I read about how Jesus turned water to wine, and I examine the wings of the guardian angels in my children's Bible. I study the Ten Commandments and write that I will have only one God and never steal my friend's wife. Once a month, at St. John the Baptist Church, I share my sins with an old man through the screen wire in the confessional: Forgive me, Father, for I said three curse words this week.

I am happy with Catholicism. The songs are catchy, the incense smells good, and on Sundays, I get to put a quarter in a tin can and light a candle to the Virgin Mary.

My father, though, does not go to church. When I ask my mother about this, she replies, "Your father doesn't go to church."

I stare at her, not sure how she manages to answer my questions by repeating them as sentences. "Why not?" I inquire.

"He doesn't go," she says.

Instead, Papi walks down Bergenline Avenue on Sunday mornings or joins his friend Pedro on plumbing jobs. Home by early evening, my father starts drinking Coors beer in the kitchen if it is winter or in the front yard if it is summer. I sit nearby with a book in my hand and watch him.

A man who drinks too much is an open secret. No one talks about it because everyone drinks. Everyone has a father or uncle or cousin like that. There is nothing to hide. But there is plenty to see.

At first, it is ordinary, a man wading into the ocean, enjoying himself. He remembers a joke he heard at the bakery. He laughs hard and for a long time. He feels larger than life, like God or the sky. But the longer he's in the ocean, the less he chuckles, the stronger the undercurrents become. He starts to complain that we're making too much noise, that we're talking on the phone too long. The television has to be turned off because the sound bothers him. The taut string of the horizon begins to waver before him. His eyes lose focus.

Then the waves come, furious and punishing, and he's cursing at me, at my mother, at the kitchen sink. We're stupid. We're in the way. We need to get out of the way. Or he's yelling about Fidel Castro and the cost of heating the house. Or he's falling down, breaking his head open, the blood trickling down his forehead. In the emergency room, the doctor stitches him up, asks how much he had to drink that night. My father grins, raises two fingers. The doctor smiles, shakes his head, says he can smell the alcohol on him.

Only one night ends in the hospital. Most nights, my mother sighs in relief when my father's body finally bends forward at the kitchen table, his forehead resting in the crook of his arm like a boy who is counting to ten in a game of hide-and-seek. He has passed out. Again.

—◈—

My mother thinks the problem with my father is that his mother died when he was born. But I know the truth. The problem is my father's godless.

Every Sunday, the priest lectures in English on those who stray from Jesus and his flock of sheep. The temptation to lie and steal torments them, the devil slips into their skulls, and then God punishes them when they die.

Unlike my classmates who conjure up sins for confession, because they are horrified at the idea of confiding their secrets to a *viejito*, I kneel in the confessional behind the dark red curtain and tell the truth. I said a curse word. I had a mean thought. I got angry with my mother. This is my fear: If I don't tell the whole truth, a fat white man will fall from the sky and smack me.

My father doesn't confess, and he swears about corrupt priests who pocket the Sunday *limosna*. But his sin—the one that is the worst—is being far from God, standing outside that flock of white sheep, alone on a hill, at a distance from where all the good stuff in the world takes place.

My mother's older sister, La Tía Chuchi, does not believe in secrets.

She arrives from Colombia the year I turn fourteen to live with us. A former girls' basketball coach, Tía Chuchi begins by assessing the players, the opponents, the court. She scrubs floors, throws out old newspapers, and empties the kitchen cupboards to find what is *viejo* and what is still good. She discovers everything: the tin rooster, the candy dish, the plate of iron toys.

"I told your mother," Tía Chuchi begins, her voice clear and commanding, her lips coated in a bright pomegranate lipstick. "I told her she has to take care of your father's things—that's his religion."

"Papi has a religion?"

"Of course, he does," she says, as if I had asked a silly question, like whether Jesus is the one and only savior. "It's Santería."

It's difficult to know whether to believe Tía Chuchi. She's not like my mother, who sighs every time I ask a question as though I were the cause of a headache. Tía Chuchi is a library. She carries fantastical stories, like the one about the girl in Colombia who was so sick that she was taken to a farm where a bull was about to be slaughtered. At the precise second that the knife was plunged into the animal's fat neck and blood leapt into the air, the girl had to drink it, *la sangre*. And that, according to Tía Chuchi, is how the child was finally cured.

It wouldn't be surprising then for Tía Chuchi to make up a story about a grown man praying to a plate of candy, because that is what she tells me. The clay dish with its rock and sweets is part of my father's religion. The rock is named Elegguá. He's a *guerrero*, a warrior.

"It's a kind of spirit your father confides in," she says. "Like a *santo*."

I consider this information and conclude that it is impossible. My father is not the kind of man who shares the quiet places of his soul with anyone, not a rock, not even my mother.

The candy dish being a *santo*, on the other hand, makes sense. In our town, saints occupy churches and hold court in front of Italian homes, protecting the families and their tomatoes. The *santos* are made of polished stone and bathed in flowers and candles. On Bergenline Avenue, they line the shelves at the botánica, where it is easy to buy miniature saint statues to receive help with finding lost items, lost lovers, even lost jobs. Like people, the saints come in all colors. San Martín de Porres clasps the gold cross with soft black hands and Santa Bárbara has a doughy white face and round chin. San Lázaro's bruised legs are like my skinny *piernas*: if he lay in the sun, they would grow as dark as his two crutches.

I add Elegguá to the long list of *santos* in my life. It doesn't matter that he doesn't have arms or a human face. His cowrie-shell eyes gaze at me like those of a Baby Jesus: curious, lively, *los ojitos* of a friend.

Tía Chuchi doesn't know about the other *guerreros*, the tin rooster or the other clay dish with the tiny machete. She qualifies her stories about my father's religion by saying, "I don't know much about these things, but. . . ."

But she does know. "They say you need a *padrino*," she tells me. "The godfather is important. . . ."

"Where's Papi's *padrino*?" I ask.

Tía Chuchi shakes her head. "I don't know. He died years ago. Now your father has women, *santeras*, they know about these things and they come and do the work with the *santos*."

"What's the work they do?"

"It's like talking to the *santos*, but I don't know."

I examine my auntie's face. She does know, but she's not saying.

I step into the *cuartico* and reexamine the boiler. The older I get, the harder it is to squeeze around the machine, but I still manage it. Now, however, I am fourteen, and I look at the candy dish and greet it silently with the name Elegguá. There are a few new candies, but this time I don't take them. I apologize to the *santo* about the stealing. I examine the plate of angry iron toys—the anvil, the machete—and wonder if they will swing themselves at me. Again, I apologize. Nothing happens, but when I leave the shed I feel that I have had a long conversation with a good friend. I feel completely understood.

My father appears to me as a different man now, not one who drinks too much and works too often, but a man with a life of his own.

I start paying attention to the disappearing days, those days every couple of months, when my sister and I are sent to spend the day with an auntie, leaving behind my mother who claims she has too much housework to join us. This is the first clue that something else is happening because a) my mother hates to clean and b) when I plead that my mother come with us, I receive a lecture from one of the aunties on the importance of Mami having time to herself, which is definitely a lie since the only thing my mother hates more than mice and roaches is being alone.

At the end of a disappearing day, the house smells better. The air has been scrubbed clean. It feels like people have been washed away from our home, like a woman with big arms used a mop to push out the nasty town official who said our house should be condemned. My mother, though, acts as if we were filming a scene from *The Godfather*. She wears a matronly house dress, stirs tomato sauce in a pan, and pretends to be preoccupied with frying *pescado* for my father, all the while making eye contact with my auntie and talking in code.

"How did everything go?" Tía Chuchi asks casually.

"Good," my mother answers. Her eyes meet my auntie's for a second and then shift back to the tomato sauce.

Once my father's had dinner and my sister and I are tucked away in the living room with the television set blaring, my mother starts whispering to my auntie in the kitchen, a low murmur like a book that's being quietly read. The only snippets I can catch are a few words about the *limpieza* and the woman saying that such-and-such was because of *envidia*.

The year I turn fifteen I decide to leave Jesus and his flock of sheep.

I am a freshman at Paramus Catholic High School, which is a forty-five-minute bus ride from my home and filled with teachers who used to be nuns. That someone could leave a nunnery is shocking. I observe my religion teacher, Ms. Langlieb, for a sign that she is tormented, but she appears tranquil, like an egret with her white hair and skinny legs.

According to Ms. Langlieb, the stories from the Bible didn't necessarily happen. "They are parables," she says, "ways Jesus shared his lessons about love and forgiveness."

I march back to my church, up the stairs, and into the ornate wooden confessional. This time, I don't have any sins to confess. I want an explanation because I have been reading my children's Bible since I was seven and I believed every word of it. I believed that dead people came back to life, that women talked with angels, and that God kept track of any curse words I said.

"It's okay to have doubts," Father Carroll whispers through the screen window of the confessional. "But don't lose your faith."

That's all he says. Not "Let me explain" or "Yes, I lied to you," but an instruction to decide for myself what is true. I thank him and storm out of the church. I will not be part of a religion that lies to me. A few months later, the fat white man in the sky smacks me.

A friend's cousin crashes his car into an electrical pole at close to a hundred miles an hour, almost cutting off electricity to parts of Jersey City. That is what I am told later, after I am pulled out of the car, after I wake up to find my body in the middle of the road, my right arm dangling above my shoulder, my left leg loose and twisted below my hip. Both the arm and leg are broken, as if God had cut a diagonal line across my body.

I know God has singled me out for punishment, because there were six people in the car that night and everyone else has minor bruises. I, on the other hand, spend three weeks in the hospital, undergo a blood transfusion (I'm anemic), hobble along for months on crutches, and undergo two surgeries. None of this convinces me to return to Catholicism. I would rather be alone on a hill with the truth and broken *huesos* than to be told stories that are *mentiras*.

My father comes to the hospital once.

He's wearing his leather jacket and black work boots, and he yells at me about the mess I got myself into, about what I've done to my body, to him, to the family. My left leg is lifted in traction. My right arm is hidden in a cast. In a few days, on my *quinceañera*, surgeons will open my skin and slip steel-like rods into my body so the bones will grow straight alongside the metal.

I stare at the hospital wall while my father barks at me. My mother focuses on the floor; Tía Chuchi inspects the bed sheet. My father's friend Pedro, who drove him to the hospital, searches for something out the window.

When my father and his friend leave, the room is silent. I will myself not to cry. Usually when my father has one of his rages, I run to my bedroom or to the pages of a book. But this time, I can't move. The white bed sheet is draped over me like a giant bandage. I close my eyes and slip for a moment into my own made-up story about a boy who loves me but can't exactly be with me, and yet in the end it all works out because really he does love me.

When I look over at my mother, her eyes are sad and quiet. My father hates hospitals. That much I know. Later on, I will learn that he hates anything that makes him afraid—syringes, broken bones, doctors. Yelling at us, about us, about the world, is the way he knows to talk about fear. But right now Tía Chuchi wants me to know that my father does love me.

"He kept vigil the night of the accident." She pauses, but this is not another story from Colombia. This is true. "He prayed with the *velas* lit, with Elegguá and the *guerreros*. He didn't sleep. He prayed all night."

The sweetest part of my father is his candy dish.

A year after the car accident, we sell the house on Fourth Street. It has not been bulldozed. My parents have sold it to another family and found a new home a few blocks away. All the holy ones come with us.

In the new living room, Tía Chuchi hammers a thick nail into the wall and hangs the Sacred Heart of Jesus. It's not a painting but a wood carving of Jesus with his white palms in supplication, his chest cut open to reveal his shiny red heart.

Elegguá and the plate of angry toys are tucked in the basement, where my father watches baseball on a portable television set and drinks Coors or Budweiser or whatever brand of beer is cheap that week.

The tin rooster is in the kitchen as always, atop the cupboard, his pale-silver eyes watching over us.

I interview two atheists in high school, not formally, but casually, over lunch, while waiting for a class to start, during group projects.

They have never had a god. They don't miss the days when they prayed, sang songs, and read books about saints. They have not walked away from the feeling that a man in the sky is both punishing them and taking care of them. They are free and (it seems to me) lonely.

Tía Chuchi, on the other hand, places her miniature plastic saints on the board covering the radiator in the living room. In the basement, my father keeps his *santos* in an old cardboard box. I watch the two of them with envy and longing and awe that nothing has shattered their beliefs. And then I take a step back, proud that I have given up foolish ideas.

The only crack in my defense is Elegguá.

Alone in the basement with him, I say a quick prayer: Help me with this exam, keep me safe tonight, make it so I pass the driving test, please.

I don't know why I do this except that the rock with cowrie shells and candies has been with me ever since I can remember, since before the saints on the radiator, since before Jesus even. And he has never lied to me.

December is the month of *visitas*.

We pull out the plastic Christmas tree from the attic and shop for paper icicles at C. H. Martin. On Bergenline, my mother stocks up on apples, popcorn, and white candles. Before Baby Jesus and

Santa Claus reach us, San Lázaro arrives. It is the seventeenth of December, his feast day, and he is crippled.

San Lázaro is also half-naked. A single piece of muslin covers his private area. He has open sores on his body and a beard that hasn't been shaved in weeks. He walks with two crutches and carries a halo over his head. Two stray dogs lick the wounds on his legs.

All statues of San Lázaro are like this, depicting the beggar from the Gospel of Luke who is repeatedly neglected by the rich man in this life but admitted into heaven after he dies. My father bought the statue, about seventeen inches in height, when he married my mother. When I ask why, he answers, "For protection."

The statue takes its place on the dresser in my parents' bedroom next to a cup of water and a picture of my mother's dead mother, a short, white-haired woman with a matching violet skirt and blazer. At night, my mother plugs in a small electric candle on the dresser, like the ones they have in church for the saints. The candleholder is bright red with ornate gold-plate trimmings. The red light shines on my mother's mother and the crippled saint with his two stray dogs.

One mid-December evening my mother clears the kitchen table of the paper-napkin holder, the salt and pepper shakers, and the bowl of oranges and saltine crackers. When she's done, my father lifts San Lázaro off the dresser and carries him to the kitchen, where the saint stands at the center of the table. My mother arranges plates of popcorn and apples at the *santo*'s bruised feet, as well as white candles.

"Light a candle," my father says, giving me the matches.

There is a *vela* on the table for everyone who lives in the house, and lighting one is our way of asking San Lázaro to protect us in the coming year. I examine each candle closely, anxious to choose the right one, the one that is only for me.

"Pick one already," my father snaps.

I grab one, light it, and then sit at the table, watching the flame for any sign of what the coming year will bring. At times, it wavers and threatens to blow out, but then it rages back to its small stature, and I hope that this is a good sign.

My father is not alone in his devotion to San Lázaro. In Hialeah, Florida, people like him—Cubans, exiles—have built a church for the saint so that worshippers can travel there weekly or daily to pray at the foot of a statue that is almost seven feet in height, his open sores the size of my fingers. A thick purple robe covers his bony shoulders. At his feet, supplicants light candles and leave white carnations and dollar bills.

When visiting Hialeah, I love watching people's lips moving in silent prayer and the bouquets of flowers exploding around San Lázaro's feet; I love that the saint's body—bruised, tortured, on the verge of collapse—does not repulse his worshippers but instead inspires grown women and men to press their fingers gently on San Lázaro's legs and feet and crutches. The consensus is palpable: only a man who has suffered like this can know what we need and keep us safe from harm.

In December, at home in New Jersey, I sit in the dark with my father, staring at the saint's crutches, relieved that the bones in my left leg and my right arm have healed since the surgeries, and I am grateful for my father's silence.

After twenty minutes though, I grow sleepy and head to bed, wondering how my father can do this from dusk to dawn every year.

This is our home: Jesus and his chest cut open in the living room, a candy dish in the basement, a man with open sores on the kitchen table, and that rooster, always that tin rooster with gray eyes, way above our heads in the kitchen, a constant companion.

In graduate school, while researching colonial Cuba, I come across a book on Santería. The word is on the cover, which surprises me. Like Spanish, the word *Santería*—and also *Eleggua* and *guerreros*—are part of an oral language for me, and yet here in this book, the words are written down, stationed among commas and squeezed between periods. They are important and real, and I start reading. And then, I turn the page.

Here I will pause.

If I could sum up the lives of people like me—people whose parents don't write books, whose aunties and cousins don't step onto college campuses except for the time we graduate—I would write our lives with that one phrase: and then, I turn the page.

I turn the page in a book and find the words we use at home written down. Or I turn the page and come across a detailed passage describing the bananas and roses and coffee shipped from South to North America, which begins to explain what my mother and Tía Chuchi mean when they say they came here for work.

Or I turn the page and find a picture of the candy dish.

The photograph shows a rock in a clay plate. Cowrie shells form the familiar eyes and open mouth. The dish is filled with candies, including lollipops. It has objects my father's dish does not, like bird feathers and beaded necklaces, and overall it is much cleaner. It is not a dish that has been kept hidden.

Elegguá, it turns out, is an orisha, a spirit, a god. In Africa, in Yorubaland, once upon a time, he sat at the entrance to marketplaces. He's the god of the crossroads, of trickery, of helping people find their *camino*. He adores children.

Elegguá is not alone. The rivers and the woods, the soil and iron and wind belong to the spirits, and the spirits have lyrical names: Oshún, Yemayá, Changó, Oya. In the stories that are told about the orishas, they are like ordinary people. They have long-standing feuds with each other and intimate relations and favorite colors. Oggún works too much, and Ochosi is at the courthouse again. That's who they are—the angry toys in my father's second clay dish, the rake and the machete and the arrows. They are Oggún and Ochosi, the orishas of work and justice.

When the white men arrived in Africa, they failed to see the gods. They beat the Yorubans, shoved them onto ships, across the oceans, and never suspected that the holy ones were heading for Cuba, too. Once they realized it, that the orishas had arrived in the Americas—the Yorubans drummed and danced and sang, the spirits came down and took hold of their heads and wrists and feet—the Spaniards forbade their practice of the religion. They thought they could outsmart Elegguá.

It's the end of the day. I can imagine dusk crawling across the sugarcane fields. A slave woman is working with a fractured arm. It's in a makeshift sling. She's worried the bone will grow crooked now. She needs the orisha Babalú-Ayé, but how? Where and when?

Someone knows. They've seen him here in Cuba, except the Spaniards call him San Lázaro. Like Babalú-Ayé in the Yoruban stories, the Catholic *santo* has open sores on his legs. And, so, the woman procures a small statue. She places San Lázaro on a table in her shack, offers the *santo frutas y tabaco* and begs for mercy. She can pray freely now and not worry about breaking the law.

It began like this perhaps: The saint in public and the orisha in secret. The bleeding Jesus in the living room and Elegguá in the basement. And high above our heads, the tin rooster my mother keeps above the kitchen cupboard: Ósun, the one who brings messages when your life is in danger.

I read more books in more libraries and learn that my father and my mother are protecting us with a divine army: Elegguá, Ochosi, Oggún, Ósun. In the religion, they are *los guerreros*, the warriors who protect the life of the practitioner and, by extension, his daughters.

The tricky thing with open secrets is that you can't barge your way in. You can read all the books you find at the library and download unpublished theses. You can visit botánicas, buy candles, and have your questions, but to be let in, you have to wait for people. You have to learn when to ask a question and when to shut up.

It's like dealing with someone's heart. You can't just knock at the door. You can't show up and say, "I want to live here." You have to prove yourself. You have to stick around. You have to wait until the other person is ready.

And in the end, you realize that it was you who had to wait. It was your own heart you couldn't barge into.

My mother tells me matter-of-factly to not be home one day.

My hours during graduate school are largely unpredictable, and she needs to be sure that I'll be out of the house. This time, I'm old enough to follow her cue.

"Who's coming?" I ask.

"*Una señora.*"

I nod and when she doesn't say anything else, I let the conversation end. That evening, the house is airy and light. A woman, I imagine, has swept a terry cloth across each room. The house feels satiated, as if the walls themselves had been thirsty and were watered.

Another time, Tía Chuchi asks me to take one of my aunties to the mall. Tía Dora doesn't believe in this sort of thing, she says, and it's best that she not show up at the house unannounced. Tía Chuchi doesn't say what this sort of thing is, and I know to not ask.

A third time, I come home to find my mother at her sewing machine in the basement and next to her, on the floor, a box with holes the size of nostrils. The bird feet scrape the cardboard from the inside.

"What's that?"

"It's your father's things," she says, not looking up from the pants whose hem she's taken apart. The box moves in spurts on the floor, but my mother snips at the thread and says no more.

When a woman arrives, her hair wrapped in white cloth, my mother tells me to stay in my room. I don't argue. I have already read about what happens to the birds, and I am not sure that it is anything I want to see.

I walk into the basement one day to wash a load of laundry and find my father talking to a woman I have never seen before: Ana. She's a *santera*, a priest in the religion. She's short, with large hands and gold rings on almost every finger. I feel at ease with her, and curious too. She's a book whose cover I like.

"Go upstairs," my father says, waving at me as if I were a mosquito rather than a woman in her twenties. It is not his usual bark, though. It is more like a pleading.

"Let the girl stay," Ana says, grinning. "She has to learn."

Ana cracks open a coconut with a large knife and starts cutting the meat into big chunks. She moves the blade as quickly and easily as if it were a pocketknife.

"Why do you use a coconut?" I ask.

"*El coco habla*," she answers.

I nod, as if I, too, usually chat with fruits and vegetables.

It is my father and me that day. My mother comes later. But for a while, it is only us and the woman, and on the floor, Elegguá in his clay dish, along with Ochosi and Oggún and the tin rooster. Ana says prayers that sound like songs, and I find myself tapping my foot to the beat. She blows tobacco smoke at Elegguá, which at first looks insulting, like smoking in someone's face, but after a few seconds it appears romantic and submissive, like a woman offering her lips to a lover.

Ana instructs my father to bring out one of the birds. It's small, and she holds it by the legs and brings it around my father who stands with his arms open. The bird's wings flutter as Ana moves the animal around his body, over his arms and torso and back.

Next, it is my turn.

I close my eyes and it is the sensation of being tickled as the wings thrum against my face, my outstretched arms, my belly. I find myself grinning and feeling as light as the bird's wings. By the time I open my eyes, the woman has slit the bird's throat and the blood is pouring onto Elegguá, feeding the orisha.

I had read about this ritual in books and thought I would find it repulsive, strange, frightening. But to my surprise, it feels normal and ordinary, like watching a Catholic priest at Sunday Mass refer to a cup of wine as the blood of Jesus Christ.

Ana tells my father to talk directly with the orishas. This is his time to make a request and share his feelings. I stare at the floor, wishing now that I was upstairs in my room. I am embarrassed. My father, as far as I know, has never been told to discuss his feelings.

He starts by shuffling his black boots, his eyes on the ground. I glance over at him. He looks like a little boy, shy and awkward in front of his teacher, his hands clasped behind his back. He makes his requests, and the sound of his voice is like nothing I have ever heard from him. This is the man who routinely screams at my mother to turn off the television, whose voice is raspy from smoking too many cigarettes and cigars, but now he is someone's son. His voice is tender, *suavecito*, earnest even.

Ana touches the chunks of coconut to my father's forehead and arms and then throws them to the floor. It is time for Elegguá and the *guerreros* to speak.

"You need to take care of your stomach," she says to my father.

From there, she proceeds to tell him about his health, and the fact that Papi listens is more astonishing than the notion that a coconut and a rock are delivering the news. Whenever we take my father to the doctor, he spends more time complaining than being examined. But here now, before the orishas, my father is quiet and attentive.

—ɷ—

As much as I hate to admit it, books have limitations.

Over and over again in the literature on the orishas, the rooster that sits atop the staff and guards us from his perch on the kitchen cupboard is described as small. Ósun's bells are tiny, the scholars report.

But the tin rooster in our kitchen looks large to me. He stands tall and brave, his silver chest wide and proud. It is said that the day a person dies, his Ósun is buried with him, and I think of the tin rooster this way, as if he were a friend who would walk with you into the final secret of this life.

I wait with Ana at the front door afterwards, while my father retrieves money from the bedroom to pay her.

"Call me when you're ready to receive your Elegguá," she says, adding, "when you have your own home."

I nod, ask how much it would cost, and say that I'll think it over, although I already know I won't do it. I don't even know if I believe in this because it is real or what I grew up with or what hasn't betrayed me, or if any of that matters. It's similar to my relationship with my father. I can't jump into forgiveness. The heart doesn't work that way. I have to gather information, take notes, observe what changes, what stays constant, what remains hidden, what can be trusted. Forgiveness and faith are like writing a story. They take time, effort, revisions.

When Ana leaves, my father sits on a folding chair in the basement. He lights up a cigar and I put my clothes in the washing machine. Elegguá sits on the floor nearby as usual, his face blood-stained, his cowrie shell eyes watchful and, it appears to me, smiling.

A Cup of Water Under My Bed

La Viejita María is a woman who looks like dried corn. Her face is a light yellow, the skin dry and wrinkled; her white hair like a husk, with silk threads pulled back and running wild around her head. She lets Tía Chuchi and me into her apartment, her dark eyes peering at me. It is the first time she and I are meeting. I am in high school and she grins, as if she approves of my height, my hair, my age.

The apartment itself is stuffed with white carnations, rosary beads, statues of San Lázaro and La Virgen del Cobre. Dollar bills are folded at the feet of the saints, creating the impression that the holy ones are grabbing the money between their toes. Apples are laid out for the saints, too, and unlit candles crowd the shelves and side tables, their wicks bent like black fingers pointing at me.

We talk with the *viejita* for a while. Actually, it is Tía Chuchi who speaks. She sits on the edge of a love seat and slips into a back and forth with the old lady about people they know from Bergenline Avenue and which priest is presiding over the morning Mass these days. Their conversation moves like a river, following the contours of question marks and commas. I try to not stare at the *santos*, because their eyes look more real than my own. I also ignore the bag of cookies my auntie brought and which sits unopened on the coffee table. When La Viejita María glances at me, I offer her a polite smile.

The old woman is supposed to read the cards for me.

We are here because I am growing older, because Tía Chuchi thought this was a good idea, because the factories in New Jersey are closing, and although I do not plan to work in a *fábrica*, I am worried about the money. No one ever told me how much college costs, and I keep imagining the worst: unable to afford higher education, I work as a manager at McDonald's, closing the store at one in the morning, my babies binging on the Happy Meals I bring home. The cards, the tarot cards, will tell us what we need to know about the future.

Us. My future is always plural. It is always about my mother and my father and my aunties and my sister. The pressure is enormous, and La Viejita is here to ease the sensation that comes over me whenever I think of the years ahead: the feeling of a fist squeezing my throat.

The conversation between the two women continues until, as if by the natural order of things, the river takes a turn in the woods, passes a small clearing.

"María," Tía Chuchi begins. "It's that we came for the girl."

The *viejita* sets her eyes on me. There are a few moments of mutual observation, and then the kitchen table is cleared and the cards are shuffled. The old woman instructs me to create three stacks with the cards. She picks one stack and places the cards on the table side by side, creating a long river of images: of men in robes, a smattering of swords, knights riding horses, a woman wearing a crown. The *viejita* observes each card as if it were an old friend and tells me what they are whispering to her: a man is protecting you, a woman is leading you, you are working with books and words, and this is good. There are other pronouncements until we reach the last card.

"Don't worry about the money," the old corn-face lady says, grinning at me. "The money will come."

The *viejita* gives me that kindly old people way of looking, as if she has already been where I am now and she has no judgment about it. I smile again, hoping that she will say more, but she only nods and ends the reading. My auntie tucks a few dollars beneath La Caridad's toes.

As we leave, I chastise myself for having believed that an old lady who looks like corn would know anything about something as important as the future and college and books. When I call the scholarship office at the local state college, they tell me they still don't have an answer. I call again and again, and the third or fourth time, the man says, "Yes," and I can hear him smile. "You got the Trustee scholarship."

"How much will that cover?" I ask, anxiously.

"Four years of tuition and fees."

La Viejita Maria. New Jersey is filled with women like her. They read tarot cards and cups of water. They swear by herbs and honey, cowrie shells and Florida water. They come from Cuba, but also other places south of Jersey: Colombia, Peru, Bolivia, Alabama, Mississippi. When Frederick Douglass needed protection from the white man, his elders in Maryland insisted he carry *hierbas* on his right side. Roots, they called them.

In Jersey, the women run botánicas, selling religious candles in the front of the store and reading the cards in the back room. They see people in their kitchens, prescribing remedies for a bad cold or a job that has been lost. They sell powders that when added to a lover's orange juice render the *querido* faithful. They do *limpiezas*, cleaning kitchens and bedrooms of bad energies with cigar smoke and holy water. They talk with the dead, with the gods, with the *cartas*, and then come back to us with messages.

The women are *gorditas* and *flacas*. They wear gold rings, gold chains, gold bracelets. They walk around their homes in house-dresses and *chanclas*. The women are black, *blanquitas*, brown, yellow. Some are episodes of *Sábado Gigante* with the volume turned all the way up. Others are thick Spanish-English dictionaries, quiet and serious. To reach them, we take the bus down Bergen-line Avenue, down that glorious stretch of sixty blocks crammed with banks, *panaderías*, shoe stores, liquor stores, and the *cabinas* to call Latin America. La Viejita María lives off of Bergenline, and so do Conchita and Ana and Juana.

My mother and my father and Tía Chuchi believe these women know something we do not, like why my father's stomach hurts and when the factories will open again. We don't visit the women very often, but somehow there they are—at the center of our lives.

There is a peculiar power to naming a person. It is unlike anything else we do in this life, this tattooing of a word on another person. In Spanish, we constantly name each other. Usually, it is a descriptor: *el moreno, la gordita, el cabezón, la gringa*. Sometimes the names refer to family roles or character traits that manifested early in life. A man in his sixties is still called El Niño, or the one who threw temper tantrums as a toddler remains El Terremoto, the earthquake, into his thirties.

With the women who read cards, however, no one can decide on a name. One of my aunties calls them *brujas*, insisting the women know nothing. "Those women are nonsense," Tía Dora says, scowling. "They're witches."

"They are *brujas*," Tía Rosa confides to me in her bedroom, her thin lips whispering because she thinks the neighbors in the apartment next door can hear. "I know they put curses on me. I went to a woman and she told me."

My father skips the formalities of names and defines the women by the work they do: Ana, *la que echa cartas*.

My mother, always firm in her practice of not stating the obvious but still discussing the subject at hand, refers to them as the women who know. When she returns from seeing one of them, she murmurs, *"Ella sí que sabe."*

Tía Chuchi nods, pulls from her pocket another story: "There was this family I knew *en* Colombia, and they took their daughter to a woman, because the girl was sick, *pero muy enferma* of a broken heart, except no one had touched her heart. But the woman—she knew. She pulled up the girl's skirt, *y allí*, right there was a piece of black cloth." Tía Chuchi pauses, looks me in the eye. "Someone had pinned the fabric to the girl's *falda* to bring sickness upon her." She clicks her tongue. "That woman knew.'"

But not always. They don't always know. That's the problem.

It is the day after. Or maybe two days after. The cuts on my legs are still open. My shorts feel like a shard of glass against my skin. I am four or five years old, and the police have arrived.

The two men are tall and light-skinned, and they carry revolvers strapped to thick, black belts. Someone has called them. Maybe my mother, maybe a neighbor. We are still living in Union City at the time, on the first floor of an apartment building, and we know everyone there. In the hallway, near the front door of our apartment, the policemen peer down at me, and the lady who lives across the hallway interprets for us, her mouth finding the words in English to describe my father, my legs, our broken places.

She can't explain it all, of course. She cannot tell the police that it had been late in the day and I had awoken in my bed, alone and wanting my mother. That I had been trying to open the front door of our apartment to reach Mami on the front stoop. The neighbor doesn't know that my father emerged from the kitchen then, his thick eyebrows furrowed and his voice growling at me to get back to bed. (She can't possibly know that the growling is a part of my father, like his head of dark curls and his bony hands and his beer belly, that he growls the way some birds sing: a low guttural melody.)

The neighbor can't tell the police that I insisted on my mother. I was four or I was five. I did not know yet that the world had sharp edges, that men and even women could shift so quickly under the weight of earlier years. The neighbor cannot explain the shock when the belt appeared, all leather and treacherous, and my father turned into a crow, his left hand like a beak snatching my wrists, his ears deaf to my screams and to the women and my mother, all of them banging on the locked door, yelling at him to stop beating me, to open the door.

I am told now to lift my shorts so the policemen can see the evidence, and I pick up the fabric careful not to graze the wounds. I stare at the men's shoes, and my mother says that no, she will not press charges. The policemen withdraw, two pairs of black-laced shoes retreating down the hallway.

She stops talking to my father. My mother, that is. She treats him, not as if he were a terrifying bird but rather a mousetrap in the kitchen. He is a contraption of wire and wood that you have to tolerate, that you glance at every now and then to check on its progress. She is angry and afraid, not so much of my father perhaps, but of knowing that there is no other place for us to go.

After the police, a woman arrives. She knows my mother and father. She is a big, brown lady with a red scarf and a wide smile. I hate her immediately. She is too happy. Too unafraid.

The woman talks to my father in the kitchen, then my mother, and finally, it is my turn. She comes into the living room and I am placed before her. Grinning, the woman begins in Spanish, "You have to be a good girl with your father. You have to be quiet and not bother him."

My breath leaves. The woman turns into her red scarf. The entire world is the red scarf, and a fire snakes into my arms and I have the burning impulse to grab the red scarf and strangle the woman, to find the soft place in her throat and to scratch her there. But my mother is nearby, and she is silent and so am I.

The words flood me then: this woman knows nothing. I feel it inside of me *sin duda*. She knows nothing. It is not a string of words but a solid and weighty stone at the back of my chest. It is as if there was someone else inside of me, not the girl with her cut-up legs but another girl, a girl who cannot be beaten or lied to, a girl who, like a river, cannot be caged.

—⟋⟍—

"That must have been Juana," my mother answers, her lips tightening.

I am in my thirties now, and she is upset that I have asked her about that time in our lives, about the red scarf and Juana, who was a *santera*, my father's religious godmother.

When I ask her for more details, my mother hesitates, as if she is opening the door of a house she does not want to visit. She squeezes her thin lips so hard they almost vanish into her face, and I change the conversation and shut the door for us both.

According to books at the public library in New York City and the libraries at New York University and the New School, I am not the first person to think about the women who know. Historians have studied these women, not La Viejita María or Juana in particular, of course, but these kinds of women, and they have found the following:

> The women engage in a kind of folk Christianity.
>
> Or the Afro-Cuban religion Santería, also known as Regla de Ocha.
>
> Or Espiritismo, talking with the dead.
>
> Or any of these religious practices mixed together.

In short, the historians know little. To be fair, it is difficult to study a subject that shifts for migration, for necessity, for colonization. It is impossible to put under a microscope a group of women who have no central authority, who protect themselves by not naming themselves, who change the rules depending on whose home they walk into.

Many of the women only know one truth: *envidia*.

My mother goes for a consultation because the factories are paying so little, because my father owes some back taxes, because it is always good to check in with these women about what we don't know. The answer is the same. "The woman said it was *envidia*," my mother whispers to Tía Chuchi at home. "But why are people going to be envious of us?"

Tía Chuchi points to the home my parents own, the fact of having any job at a time when so many have none. Tía nods her head. "The woman is right. *Es envidia*."

And so the floors are cleaned by rolling coconuts over them with a broom and my parents wash in baths of Florida water and white carnations. My mother urges me to not tell anyone our business because this much is true: any little good you have someone else covets.

Envidia is the primary way we have to talk about what we want. While my mother would deny she ever envied another person, I can hear it in her voice, in the tone of the questions she and the aunties pose to each other:

Did you hear they went down the shore?

And he bought a new house where?

She never worked a day in her life and now she's collecting. *Te imaginas?*

No one here can afford to believe in dreaming, in planning, in the pursuit of happiness. The good stuff in life is bestowed by God, by luck. Everyone knows that one call from Colombia can mean that money being saved for a vacation will now be sent to a brother in jail. Or that this could be the afternoon when the factory forelady will say, "There's no work tomorrow." Or that next week, immigration officials could show up at the factory and haul away an auntie, a cousin, a father. It happened to my mother's friend. It could have happened to her.

The good moments come to us by chance, and if this is the case, all we are left to feel is *envidia*.

—ɯɯ—

In Old English, the word *knowledge* means to identify, to recognize. It is taken for granted that knowledge is information based on observation, on investigation, on questions asked and answers tested. It is exactly what I want now.

I want knowledge that can be placed on page forty-six of a thick volume, knowledge that can be typed up, indexed, handed out to people, made permanent. Here's how you know if the girl gets to go to college. Here's how you know if she made her father beat her up. Here's how you know if another woman knows or doesn't know. Here's who you can trust and who you cannot.

My mother would not say it this way, but this is what she knows: cups of water talk. They ferry messages between us and the *santos* and the dead. They carry our prayers, our *deseos*, our fears.

Our house is full of *vasitos de agua*. There is the cup on my parents' bedroom dresser. It sits next to a picture of *la abuelita* and her long white braid, because my mother would like to dream of her own mother more often. There is the cup of water for Santa Clara, because the saint offers the clarity needed for new jobs, new *caminos*. There are three cups with paper notes floating in the water, because, in her best cursive penmanship, Tía Chuchi has written the names of my cousin who has cancer, a friend's mother who's in the hospital, and my cat who is half blind. Their names are paper islands in the water, and my auntie places those three cups at the feet of the San Lázaro statue, hoping the *santo* with his holy crutches will restore the ones we love to health.

It must have been a Saturday evening. My father is watching television. My mother is giving me a bath. I am six or seven. When she turns off the water, I am expecting a scratchy towel, but instead my mother pours a bucket of warm water filled with cologne and the petals of white carnations over my head.

"It's to get rid of *las malas energías*," my mother explains. This, apparently, is what she was told by a woman who knows.

I reach for the towel, but my mother shakes her head. Evil energies can't be rubbed off. They need a few minutes. I protest, so sure Mami will give in, but she doesn't. I stand in the tub for two or three minutes, shivering *y esperando*. The white petals sit haphazardly on my arms and legs like soft bandages. Some begin to fall off. Others, we peel away.

When I finally emerge from the bathroom, the cologne lingers in my hair. My father hugs me in the kitchen, kissing the top of my head, his lips still wet with beer. His eyes are a bloody red and squinting, and I see for myself that the perfumed bath has worked. The *cerveza* is still there with all its evil, and so is my father, but I feel better. I feel clean. I smell good. The cologne in my hair is almost as strong as the acrid stink of the beer.

This is how it begins: faith. It bloomed there that night, all *gorda* and heavy along with my doubts about the women who know. I could still hear that other me, the girl like a dark river who said I was not to blame for what my father did, but alongside that river something new began to rise up, a stretch of land and pine trees, because the flower baths felt good, because after Juana's visit, my father did not hit me again, not for another five or six years, and the second time—here I pause, I should pause—the second time was not as bad.

My father, as far as I know, never hit my mother or my sister, and in some way, the two of them—my mother with her delicate smile, my sister with her button nose—receded to the edges of our lives, so that for a time it was only my father and me, the two of us with our large eyes, our thick, unruly hair, our quick and stubborn tempers.

By the time I was ten, I decided to do what every white child in the after-school television specials had done: run away. I declared my plan to my mother in the kitchen on a summer day, and then I marched to my room where I filled my backpack with

T-shirts and stuffed animals. I had no money, no phone numbers, no place to go.

My father appeared in the doorway. His hairline was receding. He was in his mid-forties by then, working nights at a textile factory a few blocks away. He laid his left hand on my shoulder and smiled. He looked not like a raging bird or an unwanted mouse even, but an owl, his eyes soft as wounds.

"*No te vayas,*" he urged. "We need you here. What would we do without you?"

His words, all of them in Spanish, tumbled around me like feathers. I looked up at him, his lopsided smile, and agreed to stay.

The women who know never tell us to leave or to make demands. They accept that we are trapped in cages, bound to this man, this country, these factories. And yet, they teach us to make the cage tolerable. Going to these women is like going to my father, like living with a mousetrap.

The trap sits in the corner of the kitchen. You love it and you hate it. You hate needing the mousetrap. You hate the idea of finding in its arms a squealing death, a fractured body. And yet, you are relieved to have the mousetrap. You feel a little less fear when you step into the kitchen. You are not at the mercy of creatures scampering along the baseboards behind the stove. You have that contraption of wood and wire as defense. You might step into the world with caution, but nevertheless you are coming and you are going, and at times, you even feel free.

The nightmares begin around the time I am sixteen or seventeen. If the women who know are right, it is because the dead are sneaking into my dreams at night. They want my time, my attention, the inside of my knees. My mother, however, knows the *remedio.* She learned it from the *santeras,* the old Cubans, my father's *padrino,* La Viejita María.

When I am out of my room then, my mother fills a cup with tap water and slides it under my bed near the headboard. She does this without telling me, and when I hear about it days later from an auntie, I run to my room and kneel beside the bed to see if it is true. It is. The cup is short and fat and made of glass, and it is waiting there underneath the bed like a new friend, her hand open and ready to grab whatever silver shards might fall from my dreams.

At night, I lie on my belly on my bed and lean over the side to stare at the cup. In the half dark, the *vasito* is a tiny translucent urn. The water is quiet, steady. I glance at my pillow, then move the cup a few centimeters. No one has told me this, but I believe the cup should be directly beneath my head where the *pesadillas*, and apparently the *muertos*, crowd in during the night. Satisfied with the cup's location, I close my eyes and fall asleep.

The familiar images return: men and women with blurred faces, their bodies darting around the edges of my mind, my own feet running for hours but never letting me escape. In the morning, the alarm clock cries out, and it feels like only an hour or two has passed.

Everything, however, has changed, because when I slide out of bed and kneel on the cold floor and see the cup, I do feel better. I have some power. I can fill a cup with water and slip it underneath my bed.

We are a year or more out of high school when my best friend Geralen decides she wants her future read. Tía Chuchi is delighted at the news. She fancies herself an intermediary between the women who officially know and the rest of us, and it is with her that we take Geralen to see Conchita, who lives off of Bergenline Avenue in one of those apartments where the steps shift beneath our feet and make me wonder about public-safety regulations.

Inside Conchita's home, the air is cool, a reprieve from the warm streets, and at the window, the curtains billow as a breeze passes through. Conchita ushers us in, waving big arms laden with gold bracelets. I have met her before and I am reminded now that I don't like her. She reminds me of Juana, who blamed me for what my father did. It's the way Conchita keeps her back so straight, the way her eyes fasten on us, the quickness of her lips. She reminds me of an exclamation point: arrogant.

Geralen and I sit on a bed across a table from Conchita. Tía Chuchi perches on the edge of the bed behind us. I am nervous. Geralen came here from the Philippines when she was a girl. She doesn't speak Spanish, so I am here to interpret for her. Whatever the dead and the angels have to say will come through me, and I am worried that I will choose the wrong words in English.

On the table is a cup of water large enough to drown a hamster. Conchita closes her eyes. She prays in Spanish and Yoruban. She inspects the water, glances at Geralen, and then back at the water. In a booming voice, Conchita declares, "*Aquí hay una mujer!*"

I interpret in a low voice—"Here, there is a woman"—but this sounds odd, as if I have forgotten a word.

"*Una mujer poderosa que la protege!*" Conchita continues, her voice almost as deep as a man's.

"It is a powerful woman," I begin, raising my voice. "A woman who is protecting you."

"It's my grandmother," Geralen says in a firm voice *sin duda*.

I share this with Conchita and my auntie, both of whom smile broadly. From there, Conchita goes on to talk about the dead grandmother's help, the spirit of a man who is bothering Geralen, and a woman at work who is envious of her. As Conchita issues her declarations, I find my voice straining to match hers. My hands begin to gesture like hers as well, swinging up and out.

"*Aquí hay una boda!*" Conchita announces, her hands banging on the table.

"Here, there is a wedding!" I practically scream, surprised at the authority in my voice and also at the news.

Geralen's eyes widen. I look into the cup almost expecting to see a picture the way I hear Conchita's words. But the water is an empty, shimmering canvas, and soon the session is over. Remedies are prescribed. Geralen pays in cash (twenty dollars), and we leave.

We pour onto the street, the light of the day almost blinding after the cool dark of Conchita's apartment. Geralen and Tía Chuchi are nodding about the accuracy of the reading, and although I am slightly light-headed from all the talk and movement, I can hear myself, that other me, the dark river, say: I do not believe this woman.

Conchita is too loud, too brash, too excitable. She makes me want to go home and take a nap, or walk over and see La Viejita María, the woman who told me I could be a writer and make a living. She is a comma, La Viejita María. She's gentle. She smiles at me and my auntie as if we are sitting in a rowboat and the river currents do not bother her and don't need to worry us.

My parents' bedroom has only enough room for their bed and a dresser. I am already out of college when I first kneel beside their bed because something has slipped underneath: a book, a pencil, a spool of thread. And there it is: a cup of water tucked under their bed, directly below my mother's pillow.

I had expected that when I left my mother's home, my father's house, my Tía Chuchi's stories, that I would be done with the women too. It was my parents and my auntie who needed the cups of water and the *cartas*. I didn't care what the dead thought about what I planned to do on Tuesday. I had better things in life: a graduate degree in journalism and Latin American studies, shelves of books about God, feminism, and America's racial hierarchy, and late-night conversations with artists and activists. Most important, though, I had a therapist.

When I am anxious now about what might happen next in my life, I do not consult Conchita and her big cup of water or even La Viejita María. I walk into the office of a nice Japanese American woman who has an iPhone and has studied dead white men, the unconscious, and the id.

"Help me," I whine to my therapist, Cary. "Everything's falling apart." People are being mugged at gunpoint in my neighborhood and I need to stay away from a lover I can't seem to stay away from. In short, the near future lies in front of me like a series of cards turned over, unwilling to reveal anything and I am imagining the worst.

Cary nods and asks, "What's helped you before?"

Together, we make a list: talk to friends, take long walks, journal. At the end of fifty minutes, I have a sheet of paper with words on it. It is helpful, but somehow, it is not enough.

Yvette is a woman who looks like a church bell. Her copper body curves with purpose, angles on a chair as if from a tower overlooking a village by the sea. Her bones are strong everywhere, in her cheeks, her shoulders, her hands. They are made from something more durable, like iron or brass. When she smiles, it is as if a bell has been struck, as if music has entered the world the way God intended: at noon by the sea. It is hard to believe she is another Juana, a *santera*, a woman who is supposed to know.

A friend of mine has brought me to Yvette, and although she lives outside San Francisco, far from New Jersey and Bergenline, when I step into her home, the scene is familiar. White candles lay on their sides, unlit and expectant, a vase brims with red roses, *soperos* are mounted on shelves. Each *muerto* has their own framed picture and a cup of water. The *vasitos* gather on a table next to cologne and *flores* like old friends.

"It's good to meet you," Yvette says, hugging me, the church bell sounding.

My friend has brought me here because I asked. I did it on impulse, curious perhaps to meet a *santera* so far from home. It is not Yvette, however, who knows how to carry out the divination reading. It is her husband.

Carlos looks like a darker version of my father. He's *flaco* and smoking a cigarette, but he's also a famous drummer from Cuba. He eyes me seriously, then grins. He does not use tarot cards or cups of water. He reads cowrie shells, porcelain-like shells. About a recent failed relationship, he declares, "Where there was fire, there are still ashes." I shake my head. That romance is over. About what to do next in my work life, he says, "Every dog has four legs but only one road." I sigh. "You have to choose," he says. No shit, I think.

"You've had readings before," Carlos says.

I nod. "My father . . ." And before I can catch myself, I am crying, because this place reminds me of home, because I still want to know a love that does not have sharp edges.

The tears pass, the reading ends. I am ready to leave when a model ship on the mantle catches my eye. Made of bleached wood, the ship's sides glisten with glitter, cowrie shells, and coat buttons.

"It's beautiful," I marvel.

"Yeah, you like it?" Yvette says, fingering the stern. "I made it."

"How?"

"You find stuff, you know," she laughs. "I pick up bits from here and there and you know . . ." Her long fingers flutter to finish her sentence.

Seeing the ship she has created is like coming across a poem you wish you had written. The *barco* itself is for Yemayá, the ocean goddess in the Afro-Cuban religion, the great mother. I don't tell Yvette that I am, myself, partial to Eleggúa, but standing next to me now, she says: "What happened with your father—Eleggúa saw that. He was there."

My chest, my throat, my belly, my whole body it feels, falls into place. *Eleggúa saw that. He was there. You weren't alone.*

I stare at the ship's stern and the brass buttons like portholes, and I can see that for more than thirty years I have been waiting for a woman like Juana but not her, a woman my mother would have consulted, to comfort me.

A small knot in my chest loosens, and the memory of Juana, the anger toward her, falls away, and somehow too all the doubts I have ever had about these women. It was not knowledge I was seeking, not a definitive version of the truth, but rather the solace of a woman's words.

Sometimes now when I think about the women my mother called on, I consider how they may have helped her to feel less alone in this world. At least there was a woman to talk to, to ask questions of, to sit with, because no one ever mentions the silence that follows the painful moments. Everyone talks of what happened when the forelady announced the factory was closing, when a man beat a child and the police were called, when a girl realized that going to college would cost thousands of dollars. But of what happens afterwards, no one ever speaks.

It is an empty room, that afterwards, a *soledad*, and it sits there at the center of a person's life and waits to be filled.

two

Even If I Kiss a Woman

My mother and tías warn me about dating Colombian men: "*Esos no sirven.*" They say the same thing about the 1970s television set in our kitchen. "That TV *no sirve para nada.*" It doesn't work.

As a child, I think being married to a Colombian man will be like fighting with our old television. It only gets three channels, but we make it work because it is the one we have. We switch between channels by turning the knob with a wrench. Then we spin the antennas in circles, and when one points at the sink and the other out the window— past the clothesline with Tía Chuchi's three-dollar pants—we find it does work, and we have the telenovela *Simplemente María.*

Although my five uncles are in Colombia, phone calls between New Jersey and Bogotá bring stories of my charming, whiskey-drinking tíos and all the evidence for why Colombian men don't work. From the kitchen, my mother and aunties dictate warnings that over the years come to sound like twisted nursery rhymes.

> Colombian men get drunk, beat their women,
> cheat on their wives, and never earn enough money.
> They keep mistresses, have bastard children,
> and never come home on time.
> They steal, lie, sneak around, and come home to die,
> cradled in the arms of bitter wives.

The same could perhaps have been said about men in other countries, but it's easier to believe the worst about the people you know best.

At sixteen then, I know to stay away from Colombian men. I know that Julio is Colombian. But he works the grill at the Mc-Donald's where I have my first after-school job and he winks at me. While I know the dangers of Colombian men, I have also been reading Harlequin romance novels since fifth grade, and I have been waiting for a man to wink at me. Men do this with beautiful women, and those women are always happy. They do not work at fast-food places. They get to go to college. They speak English perfectly and French as well.

Julio talks to me in Spanish. *Querida, mi amor, mi cielo.* In Spanish, there are so many words to love a woman—words I have never heard before. When things are slow in the kitchen, Julio stands behind me at the register and helps me with the orders. "*Ya mi amor*, I got that for you. Get the next customer."

I give him my phone number, which is to the say the number at my mother's house.

Most women stick to their own kind. They base love and their marriages on the lines drawn between countries. My high school friends have mothers from Chile, Perú, Ecuador, and Argentina, and these mothers have married men from their homelands. Some wed there and migrated together. Others met their husbands here in Jersey among friends, at a house party, a work place. Coming from the same country was the start of connection, the entry point to love.

The women in my family do not believe in such intimacies.

My mother married my Cuban father, Tía Rosa settled with a Puerto Rican, and Tía Dora a Peruvian. They married men with dark eyes and *papeles*, men whose wallets had Social Security cards. Tía Chuchi never bothered with any man since everyone knows that God is the only man who truly works.

The women in my family then teach me a complicated formula of what works with men. My father's alcoholism is better than womanizing or, worse, a man who can't hold down a job. My

Peruvian uncle is snobbish at times, but he drives a Chevrolet and takes us to Great Adventure, Action Park, and Niagara Falls. My Puerto Rican uncle is fat and has kids from a first marriage, but he reads tarot cards and cooks a good *arroz con pollo* for Thanksgiving. Finally, God does nothing to stop the war in Colombia, but he is reason enough for Tía Chuchi to wake up early every morning and have someone to think about other than the *violencia* over there and the unemployment lines here.

My mother and aunties advise me on what to look for in love:

> A man with a college degree is best, but choose white over black because no one sees the diploma on the street, in churches, and at the *supermercados*.
>
> Forget Caribbean men. They want sex all the time, speak Spanish with missing syllables, and if they are not black, their grandmothers might be.
>
> Forget Central Americans. They want sex all the time, do not grow any taller, and if they are not *indios*, their grandmothers might be.
>
> Consider Argentineans. They want sex all the time, but most are white, have law degrees, and if they are not Italian, their grandmothers might be.
>
> Remember to ask if he grew up in the *capital* or some no-name *campo*. It is the difference between marrying the Bronx and Fort Lee.

When Julio begins calling, I get under the bedcovers with the telephone receiver. My mother and aunties roll their eyes, sure that it is a passing interest. They are certain I will marry American. Anything made in America works. The cars, the washing machines, the light bulbs, even the men.

Of course, they hear the same accusation, "*Esos no sirven,*" hurled at Americans. They even know a woman who left her husband and children for an Americano. Months later, the gringo dumped her.

"No better than a Colombian," declares Tía Dora, tucking a stray hair behind her ear. "He wanted her for you know what *y nada más*."

But it is the Colombian men that my mother and aunties knew best. In our kitchen, they are the guiltiest.

Julio is a paradox for my family. He has hazel eyes and pale skin and looks more American than the Italians who run my mother's factory. He calls my mother Doña and returns from fishing trips with trout for my father. My mother is suspicious; my father delighted about the free seafood.

Six months later, my tías and mother don't know what to say. The last time a woman in our family dated a Colombian was almost two decades earlier in a country where that was the only choice. My mother gives me an accusatory look that calls to mind the writings of Achy Obejas: "We came all the way from Colombia so you could date this guy?"

I continue dating Julio, however, because I am confident in the love of the women in my family. Despite their dictates about men, my mother and aunties teach me that our primary ties are to each other as women. The four of them rely on each other for the cleaning, the shopping, the respite of a good *chisme*. It's a woman who will fry you a good salty *bistec*, and it's a woman, a sister, who has now pulled out the sofa bed in the living room, because Tía Rosa's husband left and a commuter van hit her on Kennedy Boulevard, leaving my auntie in the middle of the street like a mashed-up bird. She's been released from the hospital and has come to live with us.

In a home run by women, I hold high court. The three aunties have no children of their own, and as the first born to my mother, I am *la consentida* and also their American brat. National identity can carry many meanings; in our home, it is a get-out-of-jail-free card that extends to dating a Colombian man. Everyone—my mother, my tías, and even me—we blame my transgressions on my American side.

My own concerns, though, have to do with another border. I am a virgin, and Julio has said he will wait until I am ready. I expect to be ready soon.

The women in my family do not talk to me about sex, and women's magazines do not mention poverty or race. My mother and tías tell me that men either work for you or they do not. Romance happens between seven and nine in the evening on Spanish soap operas. Sex comes later.

But at the library, I read the truth about multiple orgasms in *Cosmo*. I rely on a library copy of Judy Blume's novel *Forever* to tell me I can have sex with a boy and not marry him. Something can happen between a broken hymen and baby showers. College and a career, of course, but mostly it will be a lot of sex. My best friend and I spend our teenage summers reading Judith Krantz novels and watching porn videos from her father's collection. We see that women can have sex in swimming pools and hotel rooms and even on a spaceship. They can do it with different men and with each other. I observe this, analyze it, and come to my final conclusion: sex is good.

By the time I watch women have sex with each other on my friend's nineteen-inch TV set, I have already heard about women like them.

I am ten years old and sitting at the kitchen table when a friend of my mother's tells her and the tías the latest *chisme*: a woman they all know from the neighborhood has left her husband and children to be with another woman. Gasps make their way around the kitchen table where *café con leche* is being served.

"Can you believe it?"

"She's that way?"

"I never would have thought it!"

Everyone is shocked that a woman was so moved by love that it flung her into the arms of another woman. I, for one, find it terribly romantic. It's like a Harlequin romance novel but without the stoic, rich guy, or like *Romeo and Juliet* but without the suicides. Two women in love confirms for me that there is a love that can push you beyond what everyone else says is possible.

I am also not sure why the women in my family are so startled about a woman going off with another *mujer*. Besides discussing how Colombian men don't work, all we ever do at home is talk about women.

There are two types of women in this world. The telenovela one is a fair-skin lovely who works as a maid, suffers public humiliations, and marries her well-to-do man in the last episode. Then, there is Iris Chacón.

On Saturdays, my family gathers to watch a variety show on Spanish-language television, where Iris Chacón is all sequined thong and big brown ass, and salsa is a side note. She is a curve of glitter on the screen, an exaggeration turned into art of what it means to be a woman, and we are very much in love with her. Or at least, my father and I are.

My mother and tías talk endlessly about Iris Chacón.

"Look at her *tetas!*"

"*Qué grandes, no?*"

"And her backside!"

"*Cómo lo mueve!*"

They discuss other dancers and performers, debating who has silicone implants and fake behinds. I stare at the screen, wondering how real Iris Chacón is.

"She might as well wear nothing!" my mother declares, as if to chastise us for looking.

My father and I nod but keep our eyes on the screen, grateful that the reception is good on the old television set.

—◊◊◊—

After a year of dating, I am very much in love with Julio, his old white Camaro with its black doors, and the tender way he kisses me. He takes me down the shore at night when the world is flooded with stars and the sound of crashing waves, and life feels so much bigger than what I ever imagined. I am seventeen and in love.

I am also beginning to resent my mother and tías for finding any fault in a man who takes me to the movies, the mall, and up-scale versions of McDonald's, like Houlihans. The more they raise their dark eyebrows and ask if Julio ever plans to attend college and amount to anything more than a fast-food job, the more I call him and tell him I will love him forever.

Sex is a different matter.

Growing up in a small town where love easily means nine months of *gordura* and no high school graduation, I am deter-mined not to become a teenage mother. I tell Julio that sex be-tween us shall happen after my high school graduation, when I am on my way to college with a four-year scholarship.

I then go about sex like the overachiever from a working-class home I truly am. First, I start taking the pill. Then, I drag Julio to the local clinic to be tested for HIV. There, I carefully read the pamphlets on STDs and abortions. I pepper the coun-selor with questions. I check the expiration dates on the con-doms and examine the rubbers for visible signs of tears. Finally, I am ready.

Sex with a man is like what I have read in books and *Glamour*. There is suspense and need, an aching and much throbbing. There is *el* spot, and when Julio touches it, I understand immedi-ately that this is the reason women cheat on their men, risk their corporate jobs, and abandon their children. And that Judy Blume was right, too. Something else could happen.

By the time I start wearing a fake gold chain that proclaims "Julio [heart] Daisy 2-14-91," my mother and aunties refuse to speak to him. It only makes me want him more. At nineteen, I move in with him, setting up our home in a basement apartment while commuting to college and working two part-time jobs. I love Julio against all odds, but mostly against the wishes of my mother and tías.

When we break up a year later, Julio says my mother was right. He feared what she desired: that I would leave him for the guy with more money and a better car. Guilt-ridden, I tell him he's wrong. The other guy understands me better. He's also in college and a writer.

But Julio is right. The other guy does have a better car. He didn't emigrate from Colombia and he has the money to attend college. He's not Italian, but his grandmother is.

How did I end up heeding my mother's warnings? Were the romance novels wrong? Does love follow the lines of race and class?

To the degree that I am disturbed, my mother and tías are delighted. Finally, I am listening to them. I am in college, living back home, working part-time at a newspaper, and dating a gringo.

The sign in the student center at William Paterson College reads "Workshop on Sexuality for Women * Hosted by the Feminist Collective."

I would like to say now that the afternoon, which changed my life, was cinematic. But it wasn't. One night, I was in the arms of my new boyfriend; the next afternoon, I was sitting in a carpeted room with other college girls, giggling, fully clothed, drawing portraits of our vulvas.

The facilitator, a woman from Planned Parenthood, is genuinely cheerful and unfazed by our work. "That's it everyone! You're doing great!" she calls out. "Fanny, that's beautiful! I love the colors. Keep going! We've got crayons for everyone! Don't be shy."

I glance up and down the table. All the women are drawing vulvas in startling shapes and colors and spending time on the size and details of their clitorises. So engrossed in staring, I almost don't hear the Latina sitting next to me when she starts talking.

Fanny is the president of the Feminist Collective and she's encouraging me to attend the group's weekly lunch meetings. I nod politely, but I'm too preoccupied with the portrait of another woman's vulva, which looks like strawberries that have been plucked, washed, and pried opened.

Fanny introduces me to the white woman sitting next to her, saying, "This is my girlfriend."

Maybe it's the rich colors of all those vulvas in one room or the slow and purposeful way she says "girlfriend," but I understand her immediately. And as I nod at Girlfriend, I think, "I have never met one." A lesbian.

Lesbians happen on television like Iris Chacón. They belong to another country. The idea of actually kissing a girl has never occurred to me. As Fanny and Girlfriend peck each other ever so lightly on the lips, I feel so embarrassed and enthralled that I frantically look around for a place to put my eyes. Finding nothing, I stare down at the crayon drawings of their vulvas.

What is wrong with me? *Qué me pasa?* Why had it never occurred to me? A girl. I love kissing boys, but a girl. I could kiss a girl. The facilitator passes by, murmuring, "Daisy, why don't you add some colors, open it up."

I look down and it's there for the whole world to see: my vulva. I have drawn a small brown mound, a little hill speckled with black ants for curls.

Not sure of where to meet a girl I can kiss, I head for the weekly meetings of the Feminist Collective. I dress in what I think are my best plaid shirts, but instead of meeting a girl, I find myself immersed in women's rights. We talk about sexual abuse, organize our school's Take Back the Night, and analyze the importance of lube. The women's studies professor gives us impromptu talks about the fluidity of gender identity and desire, and it is all I can do to sit still next to the girl who looks like a boy.

It is the mid-nineties and multicultural everything is in. I have the books, the teachers, and the new friends to teach me that being queer is about as normal as me being a Latina at a predominantly white college. Sure, Latinas and queers are outnumbered, but now the laws are on our side, and we have a small but visible community.

The more I listen to Fanny talk about her life with a woman, the more comfortable I also feel. She knows about Audre Lorde and *arroz con frijoles*, and she throws a Spanish word into the conversation every now and then. She is close enough to remind me of home, the equivalent of my mother and aunties in one woman, with the lesbian and feminist parts added.

The worst part about trying to date women is that I don't have my mother's warnings. There is no indicator if I am doing it right or wrong. And so, my queer friends and the spoken-word artists in New York are my teachers, and they know the formula.

Sleep with your friend, sleep with her friend.

Break up and get back together again.

Write her a poem, show her the piers, pretend you want
    less than you do.

One-night stands, one-night nothing.

You'll see her at Henrietta's again and again.

My friend is Dominican, and she reminds me of Iris Chacón. When we make love, I can't tell what's more exciting: her large, naked breasts against my own B-cup–sized ones or the inversion afterwards of gender roles. I am now the one buying dinner, picking up the flowers, driving us upstate. Every time she mixes Spanish and English in the same sentence, a part of myself collapses into what I am sure is eternal love.

Within months, however, the relationship sours. So, I try dating another friend. She e-mails that she isn't interested.

I go out with a Puerto Rican butch, who drinks about as many Coronas as my father. My mother and aunties would be horrified. I am too, after two months.

I meet another Dominican femme, but this one drives an SUV, has her hair straightened once a week, and keeps a butch lover in the Bronx. After three times in bed, I get tired of being on top.

Dating a transgender man, I get tired of being on the bottom.

I go back to what I know and try dating a Colombian woman. But she lives across the Hudson River and doesn't have a phone with long distance.

I persevere though—drinking flat Diet Coke at lesbian bars and giving women my phone number—because I do not believe my mother. I have read the romance novels, seen the movies, and heard the songs. Love will work no matter what job I have, what nationality I claim, or what street I want to live on. It will work even if I kiss a woman.

And it does.

For a few months, I fall in love with a dark-haired woman who has a way of tilting her bony hip that gives her ownership of the room. Men hit on Lisette and she snaps, "I don't think my girlfriend would appreciate that." She is the most feminine woman I have dated (hours are spent dabbing eye shadow in multiple directions), but also the most masculine. She carries my bags, buys me overpriced jeans, leans in to kiss me. She talks to me about the films she will make one day and the books I will write. She follows me into the dressing room at Express and whispers that she wants to go down on me right there. "I like it when you scream," she tells me in bed. "I need you to do it like this morning. Scratch my back when I'm fucking you."

I had heard those lines before from men and from women, but it's different this time. I am sure I will never date anyone else ever again.

When she breaks up with me (yes, by e-mail), I don't know if I am crying over her or because I can't talk about it with Mami and Tía Chuchi and Tía Dora and Tía Rosa, the first women I loved. Instead, I tell them it is the rigors of graduate school that now make me sob in my mother's arms in the middle of a Tuesday afternoon.

After another night of crying about lost love, I call my mother into my bedroom. Unsure of where to begin, I choose the logical. "Mami," I begin in Spanish, "it's been a long time since I've had a boyfriend."

She nods and gives me a small smile.

I look at the pink wall of the bedroom I have in my parent's home, the writing awards, the Ani DiFranco CDs, the books. "*Estoy saliendo con mujeres.*" I'm dating women.

Her mouth opens, but no sound comes out. She covers her heart with her right hand in a pose similar to the one of the Virgin Mary that hangs over the bed she shares with my father.

"Mami, are you ok?"

"*Ay, Dios mío.*"

When she doesn't say anything else, I fill the silence between us with a concise history of the LGBT, feminist, and civil right movements, which combined have opened the door to higher education, better laws, and supportive communities of what would be otherwise marginalized people. "It's because of how hard you worked to put me through school that I am fortunate enough to be so happy and make such good decisions for myself."

By this time, my mother is hyperventilating and fanning herself with her other hand. She stammers, "I've never heard of this. This doesn't happen in Colombia."

"You haven't been in Colombia in twenty-seven years."

"But I never saw anything like this there."

—✺—

In the days that follow, Tía Chuchi accuses me of trying to kill my mother.

We're on the phone. She's at Tía Dora's apartment. As if it's not enough that I am murdering my mother, Tía Chuchi adds with grim self-satisfaction: "It's not going to work, *sabes?* You need a man for the equipment."

For this, I am ready. I am not being sassy. I really do believe she doesn't know and that I can inform her. "Tía, you can buy the equipment."

She breaks out into a Hail Mary and hangs up the phone.

My mother develops a minor depression and a vague but persistent headache. She is not well, the tías snap at me.

"Don't say anything to her!" barks Tía Dora over the phone. "The way this woman has suffered I will never know."

But she wants me to know.

Tía Dora stops talking to me. She throws away a gift from me because she can see that the present (a book on indigenous religions in Mexico) is my way of trying to convert her to loving women. Tía Chuchi begins walking into the other room when I arrive home. Tía Rosa alludes to the vicious rumors the other two aunties have started about me. "It's terrible," she says, and then: "*Siéntate, siéntate.* I made you *buñuelos* just the way you like. Are you hungry?"

Tía Rosa still complains about the back pains from the accident of years before, but she is living in her own apartment again. In her sixties now, she is a short, robust woman with thick eyeglasses and hair the color of black ash. Her husband is long gone, and since the bed is half empty, Tía Rosa has covered the mattress with prayer cards. Every night, she lies down on that blanket made of white faces, gold crosses, and pink-rose lips.

That my romantic choices could upset my mother and tías had been a given since high school. A lot can be said about a woman who dates the wrong man. But dating the same sex or dating both sexes has no explanation.

My mother now is hurt. More than anything, she is bruised, and she wonders what she did wrong. "This isn't what we expected," she says quietly one day as we walk toward Bergenline Avenue to catch the bus.

I keep thinking that if only I could tell my mother how it works with women, she would understand. The problem is I don't know.

The closest I have to an explanation is a Frida Kahlo painting titled *The Two Fridas*, where the artist is sitting next to her twin who holds her heart, an artery, and a pair of scissors. That is how I feel about loving women. They can dig into you and hold the insides of you, all bloodied and smelly, in their hands. They know you like that. But this is nothing I can say to my mother.

I miss the conversations now. More than anything, I long for the days when I came home to report that Julio had given me flowers or promised to take me to Wildwood. We have, my family and me, including my father (who demanded to know if Julio was gay the whole time), settled into a region called "Don't Ask, Don't Tell." And it is hard, I imagine, for people who have not experienced this to understand the weight of that silence and how the absence of language can feel like a death.

Often when my mother tells me about those early days in her relationship with my father, she mentions the *postres*.

"He would bring pastries from the bakery," she recalls, smiling and then adding with a warning, "That's how they get you."

Kristina does it with *dulce de leche*.

Our first date is a month after September 11. The city is struggling to be normal. The subways are running and the *New York Times* is publishing its "Portraits of Grief." Kristina and I eat burritos on Christopher Street and walk to the piers. In the summers, brown butches and black divas light up the area, their bodies pretzeled around their loves and friends and strangers, but tonight the piers are empty, muted, *solitos*. With the bone skeleton

of lower Manhattan near us and Jersey's lights across the river,
Kristina and I kiss for the first time.

She's mixed: white, Chicana, Californian, New Mexican. She
reminds me of the women in my family, the shape of their bodies,
ni gorda ni flaca. It's how quick she lights up when I say, "I've got
chisme," and the way she talks to her mother on the phone and
then laughs and says to me: "I'm on hold. Walter Mercado's on."

This is our routine: I take a bus from Jersey, then switch to the
1 train. She meets me at the stop near her apartment in the Bronx.
We make love. Afterwards, Kristina rolls over on her side and asks,
"You want some ice cream?"

She dresses and crosses the street to the deli for small cups
of *dulce de leche*. I eat the cold caramel on her sofa, my head on
her shoulder, crying into the *helado*, because Halle Berry has won
the Oscar.

My mother would like Kristina. She would probably like her
more than she likes me. Kristina believes in diplomacy. Like my
mother, she doesn't see why I need to write about sexuality. She
values privacy. My mother would appreciate that.

When Kristina and I break up, almost five years after we first ate
dulce de leche together, I call Tía Chuchi to deliver the news. "We've
ended," I say in Spanish. "For good this time."

I don't know what to expect from my auntie, but I'm figuring
she will say something along the lines of good riddance. Instead,
she exclaims, "That's why you're taking the martial arts class!"

"What?"

"That's why you're taking martial arts. I knew this woman
who rented a room once from a lady and it turned out the lady
was, *tu sabes*, gay." The lesbian had terrible fights with her part-
ner. "It was horrible," my auntie recalls, as if she had been in the
room when the arguments exploded. "They threw pots and pans
at each other and fought with their fists." Tía sighs. "It's good
you're taking the martial arts classes to defend yourself."

I start laughing and crying, because my ex-girlfriend couldn't face a kitchen mouse let alone strike another woman, because I loved her so much and walked away, because I glimpse in my tía's words some deeper emotion, some love that struggles to be steady even when it hurts.

Queer Narratives

The teenagers file into the classroom, an army of baggy jeans and stiff hair, acrylic nails and cell phones. They number at least thirty, maybe forty. Their teacher is forcing them to be here, because a community organization has sent me to talk to them about what it means to be a part of the lesbian, gay, bisexual, and transgender community. The idea is that the more contact young people have with queers, the less likely they will be to hate us or worse.

"I'm bisexual," I start. "It's like you like vanilla and chocolate ice cream, but not at the same time." I score a few smiles and half of a laugh, the kind you get when the joke was that bad. The boys in the front pause from scanning their cell phones.

As I talk, photographs of my life migrate around the classroom: aunties gathered around me at a birthday cake, my mother beaming next to me at college graduation. The boys hand the photos off like baseball cards they already own; the girls cradle them with the tips of their nails, careful to not leave any kind of *mancha*.

A girl raises her hand. She's at the back of the room and reminds me of myself when I was in high school (the big earrings, the acrylic *uñas*, the long hair tucked behind her ear). She asks, "Do you want to marry a guy or a girl?"

I want to tell her: "Girlfriend, I'd be happy to meet someone I like as much as my cat." But I can't say that, because these are teenagers. They are impressionable. They're young. If I give them the wrong response, they might beat up a queer kid one day or not come out of the closet themselves. "For me, gender doesn't matter," I announce, painfully cheerful. "I'm attracted to who the person is on the inside."

The moment the words are out of my mouth, I cringe. What I have said is bullshit and the girl knows it and I know it and so does everyone else in the room. It does matter—gender, sexuality, desire, all of it. If it didn't, I wouldn't be here talking about it, and Gwen Araujo would still be alive.

Looking at pictures of Gwen, it is her eyes you notice first. Dark and almost arrogant, her eyes seem to leave behind the rest of her, as if the face and body are expendable and all that matters are the verses inscribed in pupils and irises, false eyelashes and arched eyebrows.

But the shape of a poem counts and the body, too, so in 2004, I traveled to the small town outside of San Francisco, where Gwen had grown up. I was writing a magazine article about her life and what had happened before and after. The facts were these: Gwen had been born in 1985 to a Chicana mother. She had been born a boy. The flat chest, the flaccid penis, the narrow hips—these were not body parts to Gwen but chapters in a book that made her cry.

She tried to defy the narrative of her body like so many before her. She wore pearls as a child. I can imagine her like that, her brown face smiling, her skinny shoulders pushed back, the pearls gleaming from her neck. She's waltzing through the kitchen, a Chicano son in pearls, wanting the women who love her—her mother, her sister—to approve of her.

Later, as a teenager, Gwen applied mascara and eyeliner and eye shadow. She grew her hair, wore it in a bob. She painted her nails. She borrowed her mother's peasant blouse. The question of "Do you want to marry a girl or a boy?" was for Gwen "Are you a girl or a boy?"

—⁂—

One of the first times I realize you can love people the same way the sky in Cuba looks—without the interruptions of skyscrapers, without the boundaries of right and wrong, girl and boy—it is because people are dying.

It is 1989. I'm in eighth grade and the science teacher is subjecting us to another lesson about AIDS. For the last year or two, it's been this way. Maybe it hasn't gone on that long, but it does feel that whenever we walk into our science class at St. John the Baptist School, the teacher has written the words "AIDS" vertically on the blackboard and what the acronym stands for: Acquired Immune Deficiency Syndrome.

It is no small task to talk about HIV and AIDS in a Catholic school, and our science teacher sticks to the facts: the virus wreaks havoc on the immune system, you can't get it from being in a room with a person who has it, and scientists think it started with monkeys in Africa. We know, however, that the virus has to do with gay people and not having your clothes on, but we can't ask our science teacher about that. It would embarrass her and us, and we have to see her every weekday, which is why God invented substitute teachers.

We march into homeroom one day to discover a teacher who doesn't have white or even gray hair. Miss Substitute tells us she sometimes teaches at the public school. This is code for: You are now free to talk with me about sex, because I come from the public school, which is godless.

A hand shoots up. "How do women get AIDS? They're not gay."

Miss Sub leans back on the desk, folds her hands in front of her. The muscles in her face don't move, not even her eyebrows. Her voice is matter-of-fact, as if she were discussing manicures, the secrets to avoiding smudges of candy-red nail polish, the need to file in one direction. "A woman can be in a relationship with a man who has AIDS," she answers.

"But doesn't he get it from a guy?" one of my classmates asks.

"Yes."

I sit near the front of the class, confused. She's forgotten a step. She's laid down the first strip of nail polish but not applied the base. She's forgotten that a person has to choose. Boy. Girl. A choice has to be made.

A hand rises, my hand perhaps. "How can he get it from a man if he's with a woman?"

"Let's say Anthony here——" She points to the Italian boy with curly hair. "He's with John, who has AIDS." She points to the Yugoslavian boy with thick, straight hair. "Anthony is married to Geralen——" She means my best friend, who's from the Philippines. "So Anthony gets AIDS from John, and then Geralen contracts it from Anthony."

The class erupts into a cacophony of "John and Anthony are gay!" and "Geralen's with two guys!" but I wave my hand frantically. "What do you mean if Anthony's with John but also with Geralen?" I ask, incredulous. "He can be with both?"

"Yes."

Anthony's and John's faces have turned into pink carnations, and John is threatening to beat up the name callers, while Geralen is covering her eyes and saying, "Aw-my-God," as the girls giggle. But I have fallen into a desperate silence, stunned by the news. *You can be with both.*

Grown women looked at Gwen and they leaned into the only narrative they knew about boys who carry purses: he's gay. A therapist told Gwen's mom that the child would outgrow this story, as if it were simply a matter of lifting Gwen from one book and placing her in another.

Instead, the day came when Gwen and her mother were both in pajamas, in bed, talking. Gwen was a teenager already, and she explained to her mother that she was a girl. She felt like a girl, not a boy. She was not a sestina. She was a prose poem.

After tears and resistance, Gwen's mother took her to the mall. They had *faldas* to buy, lipsticks to test. If her mother was able to change her story, it was because she had been schooled in Marianismo, the Latina narrative that *tus bebés* are the North Star. They come before your misgivings, your sadness, even before God.

Gwen and her mother left the Church because there in the pews, with that screeching narrative of the Bible, people refused to accept a different story about Gwen.

Some of my friends, oftentimes the ones that harbored forbidden crushes in eighth grade, are curious about me. "Did you think you were a lesbian then?" they ask. "Didn't you realize you liked girls?"

Generally speaking, gay people come out of the closet, straight people walk around the closet, and bisexuals have to be told to look for the closet. We are too preoccupied with shifting.

There isn't a good verb for what begins happening to me in college. Yes, I am meeting lesbians, but I am not one of them. I still find men attractive; it is that I am thinking of women in a new way. It is as if I am learning that I can shift my weight from one leg to the other, that I have a second leg. Kissing women is like discovering a new limb.

At twenty four, I am eager to share my findings about bisexuality with everyone, including a woman with a mane of curly hair who picks me up at a bar in Provincetown. After a few hours of clumsy sex, while still lying naked in bed with her, I decide it's important to tell her that I'm bisexual. She listens patiently, then closes her eyes, and sighs, "Why can't I meet a normal lesbian?"

I smile sympathetically. As much as she wants to date a normal lesbian, I would like to be one, not a lesbian but normal, the kind of story where you know what's going to happen next.

—∞—

Normal. That's why I keep coming back to Gwen. She wanted to be normal. We both did.

Or: I keep coming back to her, because she grew up queer and brown in a small town like I did. Narrow sidewalks, poor white kids down the block.

Or: I keep coming back to her because of the two men she met one day, Michael and José. They wanted a story that would keep them safe.

Or: I keep coming back hoping the story will turn out better this time, because now I will have new words, better words, stronger words. I will salvage some piece of her life and hold it up to the sky.

Or: I keep coming back because of what she said at the end.

Arlene is the first grown-up queer I know. She's a women's studies professor at my college and she was married to a man once, but when we meet, she's partnered with a cute butch who tells good jokes. I don't know if Arlene identifies as a bisexual. What I do know is that I can tell her my secret.

It's evening, maybe a Sunday. I'm commuting to college from my parents' and sharing a room with my sister. She has the top bunk bed; I have the bottom. The frame is made of thick boards so wide that the light never reaches the bottom bunk. Sometimes in the middle of the day, I crawl into my bed with my journal as if it's a bunker, and my mother or the aunties pass by and don't even see me.

Tonight, I have the room to myself. I'm crouched in my bunker with the cordless phone in my hand, and I am near enemy territory. I haven't told my family yet or any of my friends or even my sister. I am in one country and Arlene is in another, and I need to reach her, because silence is a terrible war to wage against anyone, especially yourself. I have to be quick though. I only have one chance to call Arlene, who in all actuality probably lives about twenty miles from me.

I don't remember now how I started, only that I told her, "I'm attracted to girls," and then I waited, and she said something kind and told me her own story and I felt less alone. When we said good-bye, I scooted out of the bunker. The coast was clear. I was safe, and I put the cordless phone back on its base.

We don't know if Gwen called Paul or if she even knew him. But maybe she did. Maybe she applied eye shadow and tried on her mother's *falda* and considered telling Paul.

A skinny gay man, Paul lived in the same town as Gwen, and late one night, his phone did ring. It was a boy in town. He needed to talk. He was gay and he wanted to kill himself. What should he do?

The phone rang another night. A girl in town was pregnant. What should she do?

Paul didn't know how the kids found his number, but they knew that he was gay, and he figured that they contacted him because they believed, like I did in eighth grade, that being gay had something to do with sex.

The young men Gwen met—Michael, José—they would not have called Paul. The stories of their lives were intact.

The movie theater in the Hudson Valley only has two bathrooms: ladies' and gentlemen's. I'm in the former; my date, whom I'll call Ezra, is in the latter. He's transgender, female-to-male, but without the surgeries. The first time I saw him was at a girls' college. He was on a sofa, and I had to look twice. Was that a girl? A boy? I didn't know. I didn't want to know. Do you want to marry a girl or a boy? Both. Neither. I don't know. I want to be normal, but right now, I can only think about curling up next to Ezra and his heart-shaped lips and munching on popcorn.

In the bathroom, I pull out a tube of black-raspberry lipstick, but when I look in the mirror, my mind leaps into the men's bathroom. It occurs to me that they have found Ezra out. He thinks he can pass, but that's not always true. Sometimes, he'll be walking down the street, dressed like he is now in a polo shirt and jeans, and someone spots the curve of his chest, the softness in his chin. They sneer, "Dyke" or another word, and he hurries along.

A woman starts washing her hands at the sink next to me, and I try to focus on my lipstick, but my mind is now stationed in the men's bathroom. They have detected that under the polo shirt Ezra's breasts are bound to his chest with an Ace bandage. They've noticed that he's using a stall to pee. They have pushed him against the wall and cracked his wire-rim glasses.

I throw the lipstick in my bag and rush past the woman with her clean hands and out to the crowded lobby. Ezra is not there. The snack counter is crowded with women and yelping children. The air's singed with artificial butter. Teenagers traipse by, cackling. The door to the men's bathroom is silent, unmoving. Should I rush in? How many would there be? Where is he?

He's here. I turn around, and Ezra is marching up to me with his right arm around a tub of popcorn so large it could hold a newborn. He's carrying a super-sized soda in his left hand. "They had a deal," he grins.

I nod and say I can see that. I make a joke and eat my tears and chide myself for making up stories that scare me.

My favorite story from the Bible is about Noah's ark. The doves and the rabbits, the owls and tigers—all of them are paired up by gender (one boy, one girl) and true loves (one boy, one girl). All of them are saved from the teeth of the flood.

Gwen must have known the story, too. She turned to her mother one day and asked, "Where does God have a place for people like me?"

—◠◠◠—

In my hometown, there was a little girl who scared me. She was seven or eight when I first met her. I was already eighteen and working at the public library near my house. She would come up to the library counter in the summer, the grime marking her pale face like gray tattoos. The dirt swept across her cheek bones and curved below her pale eyes and dug into her nose, and I stared at those hieroglyphs and wondered if it was true what the women said, that the girl with the dirt tattoos would grow up to get knocked up. The Biblical imperative of "one boy, one girl" would be, for her, "one girl, many boys."

Some of the white women at the public library may have been mothers and grandmothers and churchgoers, but they usually pursed their lips when that little girl strolled into the library, as if a fat roach had snuck under the door. It didn't matter that she was white like them. The dirt tattoos on her face and her bony arms were a coded message that she and her family were poor and were not going to be saved in a flood or a hurricane or at any point in this life, and that the possibility of the same happening to us was why we hated her so much and why the older, white women glared at her. If I didn't want to turn out like her and her family, I had to be deliberate about who I fell in love with. I want to be clear here then. I intended to date a man, a bio man, a regular man. Instead I met Alejandro, which isn't his real name but is the one we have agreed to for this story.

For the months we dated, I worried about Ezra's safety and after we broke up, I felt a hesitation when I heard from him, as though the bad news might come later. But the only news that arrived was that he had returned to his female name and to female pronouns, and he was happily partnered with a woman and joyfully parenting.

Alejandro is relieved to hear about Ezra on our first date. He is FTM himself (female-to-male), and he usually doesn't tell women that until after he's known them a few weeks, because, as he says, "If they like me, it shouldn't matter what's in my pants." Sometimes, the women continue seeing him. Sometimes, they don't. They are uniformly shocked though, because Alejandro looks like he played football in high school. He is six feet tall and has a broad chest and thick, glossy hair. The testosterone has granted him the voice of a Mexican singing rancheras. He's had top surgery, and all the cards in his wallet bear the weight of the letter M. He drives a truck built for blizzard conditions, and the only way I can get into it is by climbing up the side and pulling myself into the cushioned leather seat.

On the street and at the *supermercado*, no one suspects us. Alejandro is not trans and I'm not bi. We're simply another assimilated Mexican American couple, shopping for Spanish olives and jabbing the stupid alarm in the air to find where we left the car in the Whole Foods parking lot. I love that he doesn't look anything like me, but that he feels like me. He's a prose poem; I'm a vignette. He knows what it's like to live with both genders; I know what it's like to love the two. Being with him, I feel at home. The story doesn't have to make sense.

I don't worry about him in public bathrooms, but one weekend, I discover that it's impossible to hurry him out of hotel bathrooms.

It's a Sunday morning. It's the morning after. We're at a hotel with high-thread-count bedsheets because Alejandro had bonus points and likes room service. Some of the red roses are still in the vase. The others are in the trash since we plucked off the petals last night and threw them all over the bed, pretending a tornado had rolled through the room. We are packed to go now, but when I walk into the bathroom, Alejandro is picking up our dirty towels and wiping the sink.

"What are you doing?" I ask, a little alarmed. "We have to check out."

"I don't like leaving a mess," he says, bunching up the towels into a single pile on the countersink. I'm about to tell him that maybe he's OCD, but then he adds: "My grandma cleaned bath-rooms, you know?"

I do. Tía Dora scrubbed kitchen counters and the inside of toilets for a white couple down the shore in the summers. Now, Alejandro leaves a five-dollar bill next to the television and a thank-you note.

It's tempting to tell him that a bio man wouldn't do this. Men don't notice women's work, and if they do, they don't feel guilty about it. In general. I'm speaking in generalities. But instead, I kiss him, and we waltz through the hotel lobby without anyone looking at us twice. One boy, one girl.

Men did not wonder if Gwen had been born a girl. José Merel didn't and neither did Michael Magidson. They both liked her. They liked kissing her and touching her, and they wanted more of her.

It was 2002. Gwen was seventeen already. José and Michael were in their early twenties. José knew he was normal. He drank beer. He liked girls. He had played football in high school. But in October of that year, José was worried. Michael, too. They were comparing notes, because Gwen, who had told them her name was Lida, had not allowed either of them to touch her down there. She would also not take her shirt off at a party when they told her to, and the notion that a young woman would draw a boundary, that she would say, "This is a poem you cannot read," was suspect.

A friend made the suggestion. He was a college boy. Maybe Gwen wasn't a girl. Maybe she was a boy. Maybe that's why she was off limits. The friend had heard a story like that once. It was queer, but it could happen.

The Germans are probably responsible for the word *queer*, but I prefer to believe it was the Scots, because they had a poet who used the word in a sixteenth-century version of playing the dozens.

Back then, the Scots called the game "flyting," which meant a poetic arguing, and as with the dozens, the men would take turns at finding the most lyrical and humorous ways of insulting each other. They were considered poets, these Scottish men, and entertainers too, and language was not a collection of words but acres of soil tilled for alliterations, metaphors, and images to be slung at opponents. It was an insult at the time to tell a man his mother was the devil.

Around 1508, the Scottish poet, William Dunbar, squared off against his archenemy and called the man a "queir clerk." To be "queir" was to be off-center, to traverse or move across, to be anything but straight and normal.

Gwen planned to be a makeup artist in Hollywood. She would smudge concealer on musicians and dab glitter gloss on actors' lips. She would wake up, Monday through Friday, and give people the faces they wanted the world to see.

Even though they looked nothing alike, Gwen reminds me of the little girl with the dirt tattoos from my neighborhood. They were both vulnerable and despised, but it also takes a certain kind of spirit to negotiate a world that wants to kill whatever may be soft and precious and alive.

Some days, the little girl would linger by the library counter and watch me scan books into the computer. She'd flash me a smile and tell me about her triumphs. They went a bit like this: She had climbed a fence that warned "No Trespassers." She'd procured chewing gum with only a penny. She had escaped the neighbor's dog, the one with the pointy teeth and long growl.

I don't know what happened to her, but I need to believe she was spared.

Michael wanted Gwen to prove it. José did, too. Prove you're a girl.

They are at José's house. It's a party. It's supposed to be a party. Their friends, Jaron Nabors and Jay Casares, are also there. This will be fun. Just prove it.

When she saw the turn the story was taking, Gwen tried to walk out of the house. She would have been afraid, of course, terrified perhaps, but probably also certain that she would leave. After all, it was a party. Jose's brother, Paul, was there and his girlfriend, too. She was just a few years older than Gwen. Nicole. She would make sure that Gwen was safe.

There's a game on the boardwalk down the shore in Jersey that I loved to play as a child. It's a machine the shape of a large box with holes on the lid the size of a grown man's fist. For two quarters, mechanical moles pop up from the *huecos*, some quickly, others dawdling. To win points, you have to lift the soft rubber hammer and smack the moles in the face.

This isn't easy. The moment you hit one mole, another flies out, often from farther away. By the time the machine gives a little shake, because the game is over, you are sweating and not breathing right. The hammer is heavy in your hands and your forearms burn and you are wild-eyed and high.

I loved that game. It was like you could take everything in life that was not wanted, that upset you or terrified you, and shove it underground.

Gwen is alone in the bathroom.

Michael barges in to feel her up, but she refuses, and he's startled somehow. He retreats. The woman at the party, Nicole, says she will do it. In the bathroom, she puts her hand up Gwen's skirt, then runs into the hallway screaming, and the bathroom is no longer a bathroom. It is a tiled cage.

Michael drags Gwen out into the living room. He punches her in the face. He chokes her. José starts crying that he isn't gay.

He isn't. He can't be. He grabs a kitchen skillet and slams it against Gwen's head. She's bleeding now. She's begging them to stop. "No, please don't, I have a family," she cries.

The woman has left with her boyfriend. Two of the men, Jay and Jaron, appear with shovels. Michael punches Gwen again, and this time, she slumps to the floor and goes silent. In the garage, Michael or José, perhaps both, perhaps the other two as well, one of them or all of them, they tie a rope around Gwen's neck. One of them pulls on the rope, then they throw her into the back of their truck. They've wrapped her in a comforter.

They bury Gwen in the foothills of the Sierra Nevada. The grave is shallow.

Gwen's words: No, please don't, I have a family.

In the most terrifying of moments, she reached for that epic placed in the hands of so many Chicanas and Colombianas and Dominicanas, and Greeks and Romans and Africans: I have family, I have a tribe, I belong.

Gwen had a family who loved her, who expected her home. Her mother would later say she knew something was wrong that night because "She always called, always." Gwen had family, who if she was hurt, would hurt as well. People who cared about the story of her life. She thought Michael and José would understand this, but they had just lost their own story.

Before they murdered her, José buried his dark face in his hands and cried, "I'm not gay." The other woman in the house, Nicole, rushed to his side. "You still look like the football player I knew you as," she told him.

The lawyers arrived later, much like the writers: to construct another story.

The *abogados* insisted that it was, if not justifiable, at least understandable that a group of young hetero men would murder when they discovered themselves with a fractured narrative. *Transpanic*, they called it, insisting that any reasonable person would have done as Michael and José did, any reasonable person would have killed the girl, the brown girl, the poor girl. It would have been normal.

At the San Francisco Opera House, Alejandro fidgets in his seat, twisting to his right and left, as if he were at a baseball game. "Aren't these seats great?"

They are. We have a clear view of the stage. He's in a tux. I'm in a silky black dress. It's the first time either of us has seen an opera.

Later, back home, Alejandro will trust me with the needle. I will sit on the edge of the sofa and replay the instructional You-Tube video three times. "I want to be sure I'm doing this right," I say, holding the needle up in the air like a pistol. I will tell him again that I don't think he needs testosterone. He already has a beard and a deep voice. He can pass. The women in my family suspect nothing, and neither does anyone else.

"Enough," he says. "Do it already." And I tip the needle toward his body.

Qué India

My auntie has stopped talking to me. She hates what I have done, what I have become. No. She hates what I have said. She is upset about the words. She cares about words, about how they sit on the page and in our lives; mostly she cares about what others will say. She wants to be liked, respected. At the end of her life, she wants the village to speak well of her, to remember that she was one of the youngest of twelve children in Colombia, that because her brothers and sisters worked, she was able to study a dead man's short story.

She studied his vowels. Sitting in Bogotá, she did not analyze Tomás Carrasquilla's fiction for motifs or metaphors. She was (even at that age) practical. It was the vowels she cared about and the parts of speech and the root words and love. She wrote that she hoped her thesis would awaken enthusiasm for regional dialects.

Tía Dora is not speaking to me now. I used the wrong words. I admitted to kissing a woman.

In Colombia, and other parts of Latin America, a person can be kissed to death. *El beso de la muerte*, they call it, referring not to a woman's kisses, but to a parasite.

Magnified and photographed, the parasite appears like a pink tadpole with a tiny whip of a tail. *Trypanosoma cruzi* can, however, crawl into a person's heart and inflate the organ, turning the heart into a time bomb, so that years after the parasite's arrival, after its *beso*, sometimes even twenty years later, the heart, engorged like a red balloon, will finally explode, and the person's death will mistakenly be diagnosed as a heart attack.

In some cases though, the parasite does not plunge into the heart but wiggles instead into the intestines. There, it gnaws at nerve endings until the muscles begin to collapse and the intestines unravel like yarn. The person's belly swells so that even a man can begin to look as though he is pregnant. Eating becomes impossible.

The disease was named Chagas, after the doctor in Brazil who identified it in 1909, but people being people and needing a name that is more accurate, refer to it as the kiss of the death.

In 1978, it became clear that my Tía Dora had been kissed.

It began like a stomach ache, a fever. Tía Dora's belly swelled as if she had been knocked up. She was in her late twenties and her brothers teased her. Then the jokes halted, because her temperature did not drop, and she couldn't eat. The doctors told her mother to make funeral preparations. Nothing could be done. Ice cubes melted on Tía's forehead.

But it was the late seventies. It was possible to get a visa for medical reasons, and up north, up in Manhattan, there was a hospital, a doctor. He said he would operate.

I want to tell my tía now that sexuality is not an illness. Love is not a parasite. And even if it were, we should speak about it. We should name it.

But she would shudder. She doesn't want anyone to know that she is sick.

Tía Dora arrived in New Jersey before Christmas. It was 1980. I was five and my auntie was a wisp of a woman with a protruding belly. Her light-brown hair was in ringlets and her hands were so delicate and pale that they looked like white candlesticks. She seemed to float into the room like a piece of silk *hilo*, that's how tiny she was.

The image of a fairy comes to mind.

Dr. Alfred M. Markowitz was a tall man with bushy eyebrows and a wide smile. In New York, in 1981, he explained to my auntie that surgery was needed, that it was of a critical nature, that she and her family must understand the risks. He said all of this in English and my auntie probably nodded. She had studied English in Colombia. She knew what he was saying. She could also see that he was nervous. But there was no need to be.

In Colombia, Tía Dora had her mother and sisters and brothers and friends and cousins and nephews and nieces, all of them, a not-so small tribe, praying for her, and so Tía Dora had a faith under her thin feet like a sheet of rock: solid, black, determined. Faith was not theoretical; it was the deep knowledge that she was loved.

Dr. Markowitz had another request.

Surely, he looked into Tía Dora's eyes. She was lying in the hospital bed at Columbia-Presbyterian Medical Center, the white gown covering her thin bones, her swollen belly. She looked like a fairy resting in a meadow. He stood over her and said, "If, in any way, I make a mistake, I ask for your forgiveness."

This is what she noted later on a cassette recording for her mother: he asked for *perdón* ahead of time.

Long before I began kissing women, I was a problem for Tía Dora, and she for me.

At the kitchen table, I try, at the age of six or seven or eight, to grab the ketchup bottle, but it's too far away. "*Dáme el* ketchup!" I command Tía Dora.

She picks up the bottle. "Excuse me?"

I think she hasn't heard me. "Give me the ketchup!"

She doesn't move her hand, and I slightly marvel at her ability to not give in to me until it dawns on me that she is holding the ketchup hostage. "Give it to me!"

"What do you say?"

"Give it to me!"

"*Cómo se dice?*"

"*Por favor!*" I wail. "*Dáme el* ketchup, *por favor.*"

She places the bottle in my desperate outstretched hands and declares, "*Qué india!*"

Once a year, children here are told to think about Native Americans. We are instructed to draw them with brown crayons standing next to a turkey and a white man with a funny black hat and a squiggly line for a mouth. But in Latin America (or rather the Latin America that comes to Jersey with Tía Dora), the natives are people you have to think about constantly, because when you behave badly, which is to say when you don't do what the grown women want you to do, you are immediately accused of being one of them: *una india.*

If I am remiss in kissing Tía Dora on the cheek in the morning, I am *una india.* If I don't say please, thank you, can I help you with that, I am *una india.* If I lose my temper or want to be left alone with a book, I am definitely *una india.*

It does not matter how a person looks in this regard. You can have fair skin and blue cornflower eyes. What counts is how you speak, how you sit, how you move in the world. You can be as white as an eggshell and still be *una india.*

At an early age, then, I learn you belong to a people based on what you do and what you say.

Dr. Markowitz sliced away at Tía Dora's insides with a terrible American determination to remove the parasite. He sent her home to us. We took her back to him. He cut again, sent her home.

It was the early eighties. The kissing disease had no cure. It was only seen in Colombia, in Bolivia and Brazil, not in New York. The solution was to cut and cut and cut some more.

We took her to the doctor several times during her first two years here in New Jersey. At one point, she spent an entire month at the hospital. She celebrated her birthday there, and that day, she begged God to remove negative thoughts from her mind. She was afraid the stitches on her belly would burst open.

Finally, the kiss of death subsided. It became an embrace and Tía would not die, but she would have symptoms to manage for the rest of her life: belly aches when she ate certain foods, a terrible constipation. She was never to allow an emergency room to take an x-ray of her belly. The technicians would not be able to make sense of the way her intestines looped and dipped like pieces of ribbon that had been thrown recklessly onto a Christmas tree.

The women in my family insist that I translated in those years, that I was the song between Tía Dora and the nurse who came to our apartment in Jersey, that at the age of five and six and seven, I danced from English to Spanish and Spanglish and back again, following the music of questions about what hurts and does it hurt here and tell me about your bowel movements.

But I don't remember the melody, only that when my auntie called for me, she wanted me to be a lady. I was to answer, "*Señora?*" or "*A tus ordenes,*" and when I refused, her terrible charge: *Qué india.*

The last time we spoke was a day or so after I told my mother I was dating women.

I was on Bergenline Avenue, running errands. I knew Tía Dora's phone number by heart. I was twenty-five and I had been dialing her number since I was ten. I wasn't that far from her apartment and called her from a pay phone to see how she was feeling.

Her voice was weak. She had been sick, very sick. "Hello?"

"It's me," I said, cheerful and naive and behind me the blare of cars and buses and people shopping on Bergenline. "How are you feeling today?"

Her voice tightened, as if someone had pulled at the end of a very short piece of string. "What your mother is suffering—"

And then my memory blurs. She said, "Don't talk to me" or "Don't call me again" or "Don't call here again." It is not the words I remember but the high notes, the sense of being shoved out of a room, as well as the distinct feeling that what was wrong was not that I had fallen in love with a femmy butch, but that I had said it. I had spoken. I was worse than *una india*.

Tía Dora spent three months in the hospital that year, because after twenty years of silence, the kissing disease had returned. Her stomach ached. She refused food and lost weight. Still, she didn't want anyone to know—not her coworkers at the school where she taught Spanish, not her neighbors—because unlike me, she was a lady. She had manners. She knew there were some things that should not be said.

A woman from Colombia told me recently that this whole notion of not speaking is a very Indian concept in my mother's country. "Your family's from the mountain areas of Colombia," she said. "It makes sense." The Indians there are stoic, she added. They would rather suffer in dignity and silence.

According to this Colombiana, then, the real *india* is my auntie. But Tía Dora has always insisted that *una india* behaves badly and is loud about it.

It goes on like that, back and forth, none of us making any sense, none of us talking about actual indigenous women, but all of us instead trafficking in a racial specter meant to keep every woman of every color in her place.

—◊◊◊—

When Tía Dora stopped speaking to me, I assumed she would grow out of it. The women in my family are amazingly skilled at shutting the door on each other and on brothers and cousins and friends, insisting on some real or imagined grievance, and then months later or even a year later, some event will happen— a wedding, a car accident, a job loss—and they will swing open the door and invite the person back into their lives, as if nothing had happened.

All I had to do was wait.

Years before she stopped speaking to me, Tía Dora was worried about the Indians.

The United States had funded wars in Central America, driving people north and into our neighborhood in Jersey. Tía Dora saw these immigrants at the bus stop, at first mostly just men, and announced, "The *indios* are everywhere"—not because they had misbehaved like me but because they were short, had thick black hair and brown faces, and wore cheap jeans. For Tía, these physical signs indicated illiteracy, poverty, and a lack of *cultura*.

What makes racism so difficult to eradicate, not from laws but from people's minds, is how defined it is by contradictions. It is never one fixed idea, one parasite that we can identify and slice away. Racism, in this sense, is always moving. The problem is how you behave. The problem is how you look. The problem has exceptions.

It's true. Tía Dora married *un indio*.

José was from Perú. He was dark with a round, almost flat face, like the center of a sunflower. He looked like a man who had been plucked from his village and stuffed into a tuxedo for a wedding in New Jersey. But he was not a real *indio*.

He wore dress pants.

He took Tía Dora to the movies.

He read the newspaper.

He said, "Señora?" when my auntie called for him.

I was about ten when they married, and later Tía would whisper to me: "He's a good man."

Hatred requires intimacy. A person has to know a thing well enough to hate it. She has to be familiar with the smell of it, how it walks, how it laughs. She has to know it the way she does the sight of her own hands, thin and pale, clutching at bed sheets in the early hours of the morning.

I don't know if Tía Dora actually knew an indigenous person in Colombia, but she was intimate with poverty and parasites and alcoholism. To be both poor and sick in any country is to realize at every turn that you are expendable and that this is how the world treats its first peoples. It is tempting to think, to hope, that behavior, ours as ladies, as señoritas, can change this.

As much as I fight my auntie, I am very much like her. I don't have a problem with Indians. For me, it's the welfare queen.

She pushes a baby stroller up and down Anderson Avenue. She stands outside our local library, screaming into the pay phone's receiver. She doesn't care who knows her business. She is angry with her man. She carries a beeper on her jeans, the little black machine like a piece of dynamite strapped to her hip.

I never ask her name, but she looks like me: thick, dark hair, glasses, full lips, long acrylic nails. She wears large, gold hoop earrings.

Of course, I have no idea if she is on public assistance, but she is my image of a welfare queen, of everything I do not want to become. I don't want a baby out of marriage. I don't want a relationship full of argument, had over phones and beepers. I don't want hours with nothing to do but push a baby carriage and wait by that pay phone on Anderson Avenue.

Coming out of the library, I look at this girl, and her life feels so empty to me that sometimes I think I will cry. But instead I grow angry. I don't understand yet that I don't hate the girl. I don't hate anyone on welfare. I don't even hate poverty. What I rail against is someone else making decisions about our lives, about where the good schools are placed, where the bus lines will run, who the health clinic can treat, and the shame shoved onto us, how it crawls inside of our lives and eats away at us until all we can do is scream, and it doesn't matter who hears us. In fact, we want everyone on Anderson Avenue to hear. We want to matter.

Sometimes, Tía Dora called me *"indiecita"* as a sign of affection, as in *"la indiecita* looks pretty today."

It's common in Spanish, especially in Colombia, to add *"-ita"* or *"-ito"* to a word, even a hostile one, and believe it is made more endearing. A skinny woman becomes *la flaquita*, a small woman turns into a *chiquita*, and a black woman into *la negrita*. A house too small for a family of six becomes *la casita*, a car that has engine troubles but still bears the weight of your needs is *el carrito*.

This is what I admire about my people, about our language. We believe there is a way to love what bruises.

José died the year I began college.

It happened so quickly. A stomachache. A doctor's visit, the cancer diagnosis, and, then, the preparations. A new dresser and bed for their rent-controlled apartment. He didn't want his wife, my fairy-like tía, to live with memories. She would have a new home, even if she couldn't afford to move.

The large portrait of their wedding day stayed, though. In the picture, my auntie stands with a raised chin in her white, princess dress decorated with sequins by her sisters. Her small hands are wrapped around a bouquet. She isn't smiling. She is serious. She is marrying. Beside her, José is also *muy serio* with his glorious, dark eyes. And I think to myself that if he were still alive, my auntie would be talking to me now. Her husband would make her. He would lecture her on acceptance and tolerance. He was a good man.

It is hard to say how one year of my auntie not speaking to me has become two and three and four. But it has, and I refuse to call her. I don't visit. We have both shut the door.

And yet stories of her come to me through my other aunties, my mother, my sister. Tía Dora is sick again, she is doing well again, she is teaching Spanish to a new class of elementary school kids in Jersey City. She is going to Spain. When her husband was alive she was terrified of travel because she hated airplanes. Now she is determined to do what she should have done with him.

My auntie has one peculiar passion. I say *peculiar*, because it contradicts everything she taught me about being a lady.

Tía Dora loves professional wrestling.

She will spend hours on the weekends in her living room, cheering for men who drool and grunt and fling each other across a boxing ring, their emotions dictated by a script someone else wrote. She will shriek with delight as Hulk Hogan shoves his white index finger into the camera, threatening his opponent. She will giggle and clasp her hands as if he were courting her, because she adores his golden hair, the *bigote* framing his thin lips, his body stuffed into what I would describe as an oversized Pamper. Tía Dora, though, will declare wistfully: "*Qué cuerpo que tiene el hombre.*" What a body he has.

As a child, I used to look at the screen and search for the beauty she saw, the thrill. But each time I only saw fat men in diapers bullying each other, and there, on the sofa, my Tía Dora with her small, thin frame and a wide smile on her face, as if a bird had taken flight, because everything about Hulk Hogan and professional wrestling truly pleased her—the collection of white male bodies, the fitted shorts, the way they took space in the world.

When I start dating a transgender man, I only tell my family that I'm dating a man, because I am tired. Tired of explaining my life to my family and them not understanding, and by the time they begin shifting, the relationship is already over. I have made a secret agreement with myself that I will clarify everything if, and only if, as the saying goes, "Things get serious."

But Tía Dora hears about my new boyfriend and wants my sister to show her some pictures. His masculinity confirmed, she wants to talk to me. It has been seven years.

Tía Dora does not invite me back into her home for a reconciliation dinner. Instead, when I call Tía Chuchi on her cell phone, Tía Dora answers. "Pick your tía up here." I arrive and she hands me her car keys. "Do you want to drive?" Before I can answer, she says, "You can drive. Where did you buy that pocketbook? It's gorgeous."

"Alejandro gave it to me."

"Oh, ask him if he'll give me one," she teases.

Tía Dora has changed. She talks to me about her illness. She names it. "They tested me in Colombia," she says. "They say I don't have Chagas, so then what do I have?"

She has her hair in a bob now and colored a shade that makes me think of copper jars. She is still too skinny. "What did your doctor say?" I ask, as if we have been speaking for years.

She shrugs. "He said they wouldn't find the disease because of all the surgeries." It has been almost thirty years since the operations and still her belly swells at times and eating is difficult.

We talk some more, and she tells me she will vote for the *negro* to become president. "Obama," I say. "His name's Obama."

A few months later, when I tell her about the new man I am dating, a Chinese American, who is sweet and funny, she sighs, "I liked the Mexicano."

We both act as though the seven years did not happen, as though I never dated women, so that it's like we are speaking in another kind of silence, and I have agreed to it, because I don't want to risk losing her again, because I know that it could happen again, that I could walk out into the night and fall in love with a woman and make my life with her, and then Tía Dora would vanish. Again.

She insists on watching the new Woody Allen movie. It's out on DVD. She asks me to rent it for her, to watch it with her.

I have already seen the movie, so now I sit next to Tía Dora on the sofa, and I wait, patiently, silently, for the scenes of Penelope Cruz kissing a *gringa*. When they begin, their lips and tongues searching each other in a photographer's darkroom, my auntie gasps and covers her face. "That's disgusting!" she squeals.

"No, Tía," I begin. "It's two people kissing."

She insists that it's horrible, and I that it's beautiful. But I don't snap at her. I don't try to convince her. I don't go all *india* on her, and when I leave her apartment a few hours later, I kiss her good-bye on the cheek the way you're supposed to, all sweet and formal, like she taught me.

three

Only Ricos Have Credit

At fifteen, I land my first job. At McDonald's.

Learning the register's grid with its Big Macs and value meals is easy, like picking up the mechanics of playing PacMan. My fingers memorize the grid so that in a few weeks I am considered what the managers call "one of our fast cashiers." At the end of my shift, I feed my card into the time clock, and then stand next to the manager's desk to hear how much money is in my till from the day's orders, hopeful that it will be higher than the white girl who has been here longer and can handle more customers.

I love my job. I love that it's not a job. It's the start of something, not the American Dream exactly, because I am an American, so what other kind of dream would I have? No, this job at McDonald's is the start of the rest of my life. It is the first stop on my way to that country where rich people live and don't worry about money or being treated badly when they don't know all the English words or behave *como una india*.

A white man shuffles up to my register at McDonald's one day. He's old and his voice is muddled, as if his mouth were full of marbles. When I ask him to repeat his order, he snaps, "What's the matter? You don't know English?"

Without thinking, I twirl around and walk away, past the fry machine with its crackling oil, and into the kitchen, where the guys are peeling slices of cheese and tossing them on burger patties, then wiping their foreheads with the back of their hands. I stop at the freezer. I'm not breathing right. My hands are shaking, and a minute later, the manager wants to know why I left the register and he ended up having to take the gringo's order. But I don't

119

know how to say that I didn't trust myself to be polite, and I can't lose this job.

When my first paycheck from McD's lands in my hand, it is for a total of about $71 and change. I cash the check and take it to the beauty store on Anderson Avenue. There I spend close to an hour, inspecting rows of matte lipsticks and lip glosses and lip liners with names the colors of precious stones and wild flowers and sand dunes. The price tags are glued to the front of the display case, the numbers in thick block print: $3.99, $4.99.

The women in my family buy 99-cent lipstick. The women in my family are their lipsticks. My mother is a pale strawberry. Tía Dora, a warm peach. Tía Chuchi, a pomegranate. Tía Rosa, a plum. And I am a black raspberry. The fruit never lasts. It smudges. It hardly sticks. It vanishes when you take a sip of soda. Tía Chuchi, who knows everything, schools me in how to eat a meal without losing your *pintalabios*. "You put your tongue out like this," she says, and then she sticks her *lengua* out at me and maneuvers the spoon's contents onto it (some melon, a *pedazo* of *yuca*), careful to not touch the edge of her lips. "See?" she says, chewing. "I knew a woman who did that. She kept her lipstick on the whole day."

Sometimes, Tía Dora splurges on a $3.99 tube. Sometimes, a friend gives her a makeup bag from the mall, the kind they include as a freebie after you've spent $75. The color from those lipsticks is thicker, like hand cream.

Now at the beauty store, I choose the items I could never ask my mother to buy, because a $4.99 lipstick would make her shake her head and ask, "What's wrong with the 99-cent one?"

It is a question I never know how to answer because I don't know that what I am trying to say is this: "I'm buying lipstick to make myself feel better about the class, racial, and sexual oppressions in our lives. The 99-cent lipstick ain't gonna cut it." Instead, I roll my eyes at the suggestion. "Mami, *por fa*. It's ugly."

With my own paycheck, I buy the lipstick I want, which with tax turns out to cost something like $5.07. I also pick up face powder and eyeliner and mascara. In a single hour, half of my paycheck is gone. Back at McD's, I plead to work more hours, and when I get longer shifts and more pay, I am almost earning as much as my mother does in a week at the factory. Close to $200.

In her book *Where We Stand*, bell hooks writes about a time in American life, or at least in Kentucky where she grew up, when people did not spend their earnings on lipstick, face creams, or even television. People valued what they had. They enjoyed homemade fruit jams, scraps of fabric, and each other's stories. They didn't even blame the poor for being poor.

If a black person was poor back then it was because the white man was keeping them down. The day would come when racism would be wiped out and every black man, woman, and child would eat with only fine linen napkins and not worry about their lipstick smudging. Class wasn't the problem; race was.

Unfortunately, when the lunch counters and the schools were integrated, the wealthy black families got out of town, the white activists went back home, and the rest of the country turned around to look at poor and working-class black people and found them to blame for not having the good napkins, the kind Bill Cosby has.

Bill Cosby was on television in the eighties, the father of a rich black family, a doctor married to a lawyer whose lipstick must have been named after rubies or topaz. He was making me laugh, charming me and the country with the story that skin color didn't matter anymore. Community didn't matter. A person could buy anything in this country now. All they needed to do was to work for it.

A manager at McD's approaches me one day.

"I've got a proposition for you," she starts and explains how we can make money from the till, how easy it is, how you can pretend to ring up an order but not really do it, how, you see, it isn't a big deal. We'll split the money. It'll be cool. And I say, "Sure," not because I want to steal, not because I understand that she's asking me to do that, but because I'm afraid that if I say no, she'll be angry with me. I'm a teenager. She's in her twenties. I want her to like me.

At the end of the shift, she finds me in the break room. She has light brown eyes and a wide forehead. She grins at me, places a small bundle in my hand, and walks away. I shove the money in my pocket, and, alone in the McDonald's bathroom, I count the bills.

$20. $40. $60 . . . $300.

That's the number that stays with me decades later. It might have been less or more, but what I remember is $300 and that I had never held so much money in my hands, never seen so many twenties all at once, not even in the envelope my mother got at the bank when she cashed her paycheck.

I know exactly what to do with the money, too. Or at least a part of it. I take it to the dentist on Bergenline Avenue.

Fragoso is a crabby old Cuban who works out of a back room in his apartment. We owe him hundreds of dollars for filling the holes in my mouth. Now, however, I enter his apartment the way Bill Cosby must feel all of the time—on top of things. Here I am, with hundreds of dollars to put toward the bill, hundreds of dollars my parents won't have to worry about. I am single-handedly taking care of business.

Among the drills and jars of cotton balls, Fragoso counts the twenties. "That's it?" he asks, looking over at me.

My face freezes. The room grows smaller, suffocating. I nod my head, bite my naked lip, the shame running through me like a live wire, and I promise to bring more next time.

Although he was a part of our lives, I never saw how Bill Cosby got to be Bill Cosby, how his fictional character became a doctor and saved money and bought a house and paid the dentist. What

I knew back then about money was that you could work for it or you could take it. In college, I found out people I had never met would also give it to you.

He's wearing a business suit. A dark suit. The tie is some brilliant color, a red perhaps. He smiles at me the way Bill Cosby has done on television, warm and confident, but this man is younger. He can't be much older than me, twenty-five at most, and he is white or Italian or maybe Latino. He calls out from beside a folding table at my college campus. The sun is bright and the man is offering free mugs, free keychains, free T-shirts. All I have to do is apply for a credit card.

I fill out the form the way you would enter your name into a raffle. It is all a matter of luck. I am eighteen and I don't know about credit scores. My parents pay in cash for everything. Credit cards are a phenomenon that happens to other people, rich people.

When the credit card comes in the mail, however, I know exactly what to do. I march into a shoe store in Englewood and ask to see a pair of dark-brown Timberlands, size seven. It's the early nineties, and everyone is parading around school in that brand. You wear them with baggy Tommy Hilfiger jeans and dark lipstick, and when people dress that way, they look special, like the white plates with gray flowers my mother brings out for Thanksgiving.

The shoes cost close to $100, a little more than half of my weekly pay from my two part-time jobs. But I don't have to give cash now. I hand the woman the plastic card the way I have seen other women do in stores, as if the price doesn't matter, and I'm grateful that my hand doesn't shake, even though I'm outrageously nervous.

She hands me the receipt, a slip of paper that fits in my palm like a secret note a girl has passed to me in class. Just sign here. That's all. My signature. My promise to pay.

Back home, my mother stares at my feet. "$100?"

The question hovers at her lips, as if she has come across a cubist painting and is trying to untangle the parts.

First *pintalabios*, now shoes. Tía Chuchi doesn't know how I turned out to be such a materialist. "No one in our family is like that," she insists, and I would like to believe her.

It is a strange comfort to think that some aspect of being raised among strangers brought out the worst in me, that if I had been born and raised in my mother's native land, I would have known the Kentucky that bell hooks writes about.

But this is an illusion. Colombia is where I sometimes think it began.

I am walking down the street in Bogotá, holding my mother's hand. We are visiting for a few weeks, spending days with my grandmother and enough cousins to fill up two of my classrooms in New Jersey. The civil war reveals itself here and there, mostly in the rifles of the security guards at the airport.

As we stroll down the street, a boy my age, about six or seven, his arm thin as a twig, his lips cracked, extends a hand toward me. Our eyes meet, the same eyes I have, the same small voice except his pleads, "A few coins please, to buy a little milk."

His hand is a tiny version of my father's. It is dirty and scarred in places. I cringe, afraid of something I cannot name.

My mother snaps me close to her and quickens her pace, my head close to the fat on her hip.

"Why is that boy asking for money?" I ask.

"To buy *leche*."

"But why?"

"That's what children here have to do."

—〰—

Language is a rubber band. It bends and stretches and tries to hold in place our mothers and the plaza in Bogotá and the boy asking for milk.

In English, they are street children. Abandoned children. Neglected children. Thrown-away children. The adjectives expand to make sense of little boys having to ask strangers for the first taste we are entitled to in this life: milk at the tit.

In Spanish though, in Bogotá, there is no need for extras or explanation. These boys are everywhere. They are *gamines*, a word borrowed from the French and meaning "to steal." A boy who steals.

"You were so afraid of the street kids," Tía Chuchi remembers now, fondly, as if, as a girl, I had been frightened by spiders or ladybugs or wingless birds.

After my first credit card, an offer arrives in the mail for another one. I call the 800 number nervously, as if I were asking someone on a date who has shown a bit of interest. When the person says, "You've been approved," I feel it in my body, an elation like warm water.

The offers continue to come in the mail, and I buy a large, red fake-leather wallet and fill each pocket with a credit card: Discover, Visa, MasterCard, Macy's, J. C. Penney, Victoria's Secret. I sit in my bedroom, admiring the little plastic rectangles and feeling genuinely accomplished, because in my home, in my community, people do not have credit cards. "*Nada de deudas,*" my father declares, and my mother agrees—no debts.

Down on Bergenline Avenue, storeowners are used to people buying even large purchases like refrigerators with cash. Only *ricos* have credit. My mother doesn't even believe in lay-away plans.

At the Valley Fair department store, she explains, "It's better to wait until you have all the money."

"The dress will be gone by then," I argue, to which she gives me her maddening standard answer: "There will be another one."

—ɯ—

During my last semester of college, I study abroad in England with a group of white students from private schools. I am there on a scholarship with a $5,000 student loan and a wallet full of Visas and MasterCards. With every purchase, I tell myself why it's necessary.

When will I be in London again? Never!

You can't find sweaters like these back home.

What would people say if I returned without souvenirs?

This is my only chance to see a real Oscar Wilde play.

And the classic: *All the other kids are going.*

None of this is to say that I don't keep track of my spending. I do. I review my new credit card charges, mentally checking off why each one was required. I monitor my bank account frequently, careful to slowly chip away at the student loan.

One night, standing in line to use the phone in our student house, I overhear one of my classmates, a tall white girl from a state I've only seen on maps. She's going through her own list of justifications for charges on her father's credit card. "I had to buy the boots, Daddy." A pause. "I know they were expensive, but I needed them. It's so cold here."

I shake my head, quite smug that I would never do anything like that to my own parents. My credit card bills, and I am very pleased to say this, are my responsibility. So caught up in this perverse pride, I fail to see that I am a college student with two part-time jobs back home and a student loan here, trying to pay off the kind of credit-card balances a grown white man in the Midwest is struggling to handle.

—⟋Ⱳ⟍—

My mother is pleased that I traveled to England. She knows it's a good place. It's like here. Children have *camitas* and *leche*, and they don't wake up in the middle of the night with hurting bellies or having to steal. When I remind her that children *are* homeless in the United States, she sighs. "It's not the same."

Over the years, her sisters board airplanes for Colombia, like migratory birds. Once a year, twice a year, every other year. They hear an echo of their homeland, and suddenly, they are spending weeks packing suitcases and shopping for jackets and medications and *chanclas* for their brothers and nieces and nephews. On the day of departure, they dress in matching skirts and blazers and *tacones*, like women who are traveling on business. They wear their 99-cent lipstick and take pictures at the airport.

My mother does not hear the echo of Colombia. In fact, she has not been back in more than twenty years. "What would be the point?" she says. "To see all that *pobreza*?" My father agrees. He hasn't returned to Cuba in two decades, either.

But it's not poverty that scares my mother.

"It's so sad to see the children," she murmurs.

The street children, the ones with hungry hands and lips that never quite close.

The easy part is getting the job after college. The hard part is having the money to keep the job. To go out for drinks, dinner, and brunch. To pay for a subscription to the *New York Times*, the *New Yorker*, and *New York* magazine. To buy wine, even cheap wine, for yet another party, and clothes for it as well. The hard part is listening to middle-class, white coworkers talk about the poor and the working class, because it's the nineties and the headline is welfare reform. The hard part is nodding numbly when they say, "Isn't that awful?" and not telling them that Mami can't find work right now and neither can Tía Chuchi, and Papi only has a part-time job. The hard part is pretending you know what a 401k is, and then buying a MAC lipstick, believing it will make you more comfortable about who you are and where you come from and the things you don't have words for.

The bills arrive each month. Discover, Visa, MasterCard, American Express. Numbers have stopped being numbers. They are hieroglyphs. The due date, the interest rates, the account numbers—all these curves and slants on the page belong to a language I am failing to learn.

My mother doesn't understand how my wallet is so full of plastic instead of dollars, but the white girls I work with are sympathetic.

"I try not to think about it," a coworker says about her debt.

"It's depressing," agrees another.

"I owe $30,000 just in school loans," one confides.

It's the day before Halloween. The supermarket is selling mini-chocolates in bulk. The party stores are peddling temporary selves: angels, devils, pirates, and princesses. Pumpkins are perched on window sills, candles balancing on their tongues. And I am at the kitchen sink, wishing I could fit myself into a new life.

I have consolidated the debt, so that now instead of having a lot of bad little dreams, I have one giant nightmare, and it's in my hands: the new credit card bill. It doesn't matter that I have been sending more than $300 a month in payments. The total due does not budge.

A thread in me, a piece of *hilo* that has thinned over the years, snaps.

I pull every single credit card from my wallet and throw them in the freezer. I look up the support group a friend recommended, and when I show up at the meeting, I take my place in a folding chair and vow to myself that I will sit in this exact chair every week even if doing so will kill me.

And I do believe it will kill me to spend an hour listening to people talk about not having the money to pay the dentist, the paycheck being short this week, losing their jobs, and the humiliation of not being able to buy a friend a gift as expensive as the one she gave you.

There are other stories in the group, of course—positive tales about people negotiating job salaries, setting up debt-repayment plans, planning weddings without credit cards—but all I hear are the stories that scare me. I sit there, and sometimes I daydream and don't listen, and other times, I tell myself that I am not like these people. I am still going to turn out like Bill Cosby: rich and confident and not worried about money.

But I do what the people at the meeting tell me to do. I buy a notebook and start writing down how much I spend and on what. A woman from the group helps me identify my slippery places, the bookstores and clothing stores where I am most likely to use a credit card. I employ the forty-eight hour rule, waiting two days before making a purchase I haven't planned. I even start depositing a few dollars into a savings account. Someone from the group says it doesn't matter if all I put in there is $1.

After a year, my savings total a little more than $1,000. I sit at my computer, dazed. For so many years, my mother urged me to save, and my father would ask me how much I had saved, and I always insisted, at least to myself: *I don't earn enough to save it.* But now, here is proof that I can do it. I have done it.

I shut my laptop and declare myself cured.

—⚏—

What I loved as a child about Bill Cosby was that he didn't need help. He never had to stick his hand out for charity or even to ask a question about what someone said in English.

We were always needing help, always needing a health clinic or a dental clinic or a women's clinic. We were always needing someone to translate for us or give us a ride somewhere because we didn't own a car. We were, I thought naively as a child, always waiting.

I was too young then to understand that health care was privatized, that factories needed people like my mother and my father and my tía, that even Bill Cosby needed us. It was our work that made his day possible.

It takes thirty-seven days, about five weeks, for me to charge $1,003.28 on my credit cards, and for this, I blame the man at Amtrak.

Sure, I had signed up for a new credit card, telling myself that this one would be different. It wasn't like the other cards. This was an airline credit card. I would be charging, yes, but paying it off at the end of the month, while accumulating points for a free flight. I told myself, I'll be getting one over on the airline companies.

Instead, I find myself at Union Station in Washington, DC. I am in line behind business suits, waiting to get my electronic Amtrak ticket and feeling annoyed that I will have to wait a few hours at the station. When I reach the self-service computer monitor, an Amtrak customer representative is there (in theory) to field any questions I may have. A tall man, he is a bit older, smiling and friendly, and offers to help me locate my ticket.

He blinks at the monitor. "Your train isn't leaving until eight o'clock."

"I know." I pout.

He taps the computer screen. "There's a five o'clock train. Why don't you take that?"

An earlier train? I look at him and find myself staring into Bill Cosby's fatherly face. Why don't you take the earlier train? You're tired. You deserve it.

"How much is it?" I ask, dubious.

"It's just another $21," he says, adding, "It's not that much. You'll be home in no time."

I look at the monitor and the Amtrak worker with those father-knows-best eyes and think about the guava pastry waiting for me at my auntie's apartment in Jersey. I hand the man my credit card. He swipes it for me, and in less than a second, my reality has changed. I will not have to eat a cold sandwich at the train station and arrive in the city at midnight. I can now board the train, nap, and when I wake up, I will be home.

A month later, when I open the bill and see the amount due, I review every charge. New tires ($232.76), contact lenses ($209.51), a purchase at the Hello Kitty store ($25.05). Important stuff, I tell myself. But still. I add up the charges, confident that the company has made a mistake. It cannot be $1,003.28. It just can't. But it is. And the $21 for the Amtrak ticket sits there on the page, as if it were blameless.

Back to my little support group I fly, this time in tears. "This is just money," I keep repeating. "How can it affect me like this? It's ridiculous."

The group meets in a church room that has fraying carpet and thin, plastic chairs. Through the windows, the morning sky is gray and dull. About twenty people have gathered to talk about the same things: money, credit cards, unsecured loans. When the meeting pauses for a break, four or five people rush to my side. They want to help.

—◊◊—

I wish I could be like bell hooks.

She has written that because she was never accepted in white or black middle-class circles as a young woman, she didn't try to belong. She didn't try to dress like she had money she didn't have; she didn't enjoy the illusion that material goods would make her feel better. She found that she liked to live simply, and she hated the hedonistic consumer culture that is American life.

I wish I could be like that, but I'm not. I love the iPhones and iPads, the hybrid cars and hybrid bikes, the leather shoes made in Israel, the $22.50 lipstick, the Coach handbags, the hotel rooms with flat-screen televisions in the bathrooms, the $10 herbal teas, the $3.99 a bag organic lettuce, the Kindles, the hardcover books with their deckled edges, even the $3,000, bred-to-size lapdogs.

When I create a spending plan that includes only the organic lettuce, and no fantasy that I will ever use a credit card to buy that or anything else, I am heartbroken. And embarrassed. I'm a feminist. I write about social justice issues. How can I want any of these things? I berate myself, and before that gets out of hand, I call a friend because by now I know that blaming myself for what I feel only makes me think that buying a mocha-scented soy candle for $21 will make me feel better. It doesn't.

I wake up one morning and reach for my cell phone. I turn it on and hit a speed-dial button, but an automated voice answers me instead.

It has happened exactly as the customer-service representative said it would: A Sprint computer has shut off my phone. I can't place another call until I have paid the bill, a little more than $200, which I will in about two days when my paycheck appears in my Washington Mutual checking account. In the meantime, I have consulted with my support team, reviewed my options, and concluded that I can live without a cell phone for three days

The hard part is telling my mother.

I have decided to be honest, which benefits my spiritual practice but bruises my ego and worries Mami.

"What do you mean you can't pay the phone bill?" she asks.

Not being able to pay a bill in my family means a person is close to financial ruin, about to apply for welfare, or, worse, about to be thrown out of their home and forced to live on the street like *gamines*.

"I mishandled things," I tell her. "But I'll pay it on Friday."

She grows silent, furrows her eyebrows. She's worried and confused, because my mother is familiar with the likes of bell hooks. She can walk through the shopping mall in Paramus and feel rich from the looking.

The street children.

It's their hands that haunt me. Little, brown hands. The fingers stretched out like the basket for *limosna* in church on Sundays. The baskets were made of wicker, and we dropped our alms (four quarters) into them when I was a child, and the baskets ate the coins and I worried that we wouldn't have enough to feed them. They looked like open hands to me, those baskets. Open hands and terror.

My Father's Hands

Parts of my father's hands are dead.

The skin has protected itself by hardening, turning his large hands into a terrain of calluses and scars, the deep lines scattered on his palms like dirt roads that never intersect. It is a beautiful and unforgiving landscape, as after a hurricane when trees are uprooted and the ground is strewn with the wreckage of collapsed roofs and crushed kitchen tables, when people walk among the ruins searching for a familiar photograph, a black *falda*, a comforter, a piece of their lives that survived the storm.

I don't know why we return, what pushes us to look for meaning in places defined by loss, but the impulse is there like warm air after a hurricane.

Revolutions take time.

In history books, they unfurl over the course of three sentences, but in real life, they span decades of chaos and corruption, negotiations and false starts. They arrive late, if at all. In Cuba, the Revolution does not reach my father in time.

Born in 1932, a few hours east of Havana, on a farm near the town of Fomento, my father is already a teenager with curly brown hair when he sees a government soldier in the hills. He likes the man's matching jacket and pants, the uniform's sense of purpose. My father doesn't want to be a farmer like his uncle and cousins, picking coffee beans, cutting sugar cane, raising pigs, pissing in the fields. He wants more. He wants to be on the side that wins.

Some years later, my father gets the government uniform, and he fights against Fidel Castro. By virtue of his birth, of his family's poverty, my father is on the wrong side. He talks about it now when he's drunk too much, slurring the words and his history into any number of possibilities. But this much is true, he says, jabbing a finger into my shoulder: "It isn't easy to switch sides once a war has begun."

My father leaves the island in 1961 as the United States closes its embassy in Havana. He arrives in New York, a thin young man. He cuts hair, opens a bakery, chops wood, closes the bakery. In the seventies, he settles into factory work in New Jersey and marries my mother. He adopts the uniform of poor immigrants: black jeans, white cotton Hanes T-shirt. He keeps his hands busy. There is work, yes, but there are also cigars, cigarettes, and cans of beer.

He returns to visit Cuba eighteen years later, in 1979, and brags to his cousins about how good work is in the North. His job is to stay up through the night with a textile machine. He doesn't need more than a few English phrases. He is at the factory ten or twelve hours each weeknight and sometimes Saturdays, too.

For the *fábricas*, however, it is the beginning of the end.

Textile machines are like doll houses. They can be opened and closed, their contents manipulated, their rooms turned into theater stages. My father's job at the factory is to manage the doll house.

In one room of the house, a dance happens at a ferociously fast speed. It is a choreographed *baile*. The machine's large steel needles line up before an equal number of spools of thread. The needles pull the dark blue thread, spin and sweep their partners, tuck them here and there. It is a raucous dance. After a short time, the sound of the needles, of that steel machinery tapping its feet, scrapes the ear.

In another room of the doll house, a stiff sheet of fabric is emerging, and the machine's fingers spin the fabric like a woman on the dance floor into bundles as tall as my father.

My father keeps the dance going in one room, replacing broken needles and naked spools, and he carries the bundles of fabric into another room, where they are loaded onto trucks.

He arrives at the factory in the evening, and he emerges the next day as the sun rises. He walks a few blocks home, crawls into bed, pulls the sheets over his ears and head, and his hands reach for my mother. The two of them stay up, whispering until my mother rises, wakes my sister and me, and prepares for her day at a different factory. There, she spends the hours stitching pre-cut sleeves to box-shaped sweaters. She keeps her foot on the pedal, her hands carefully pushing the fabric under the stabbing point of the needle. When she's done with a piece, she tosses the sweater in a box. Another woman will cut the ends of the *hilo*.

When two people have been close, you can say in Spanish that they were fingernails and dirt. *Eran uña y mugre.* That's how close they were.

My father and I are not like that. His hands are too dangerous. They open a beer can and then another. They yank the telephone cord until it snaps from the jack in the wall. They poke my shoulders and slap the back of my head and pull me into hugs that stink of vodka and dirt.

In the late eighties, the world begins to shift. It happens at first in comments. My mother hears from women on the bus that they have found work as home attendants and that it's not so bad. Most days. You convince the old people to eat their microwave dinners and later you lift them onto the toilet. Most of the time, the *viejos* are only grouchy. Sometimes, they turn disrespectful. But you can quit and find another old person to care for.

Tía Chuchi leaves one factory, but can't find work at another. She knocks on doors, calls old friends. No one is hiring. Finally, she signs up for state training and starts working at a day-care center. She comes home, exasperated. "There's two of us and twenty children," she complains, opening a bag of crackers next to her shelf of miniature saints. "You tell me: How is that fair to anybody?"

For my father, the loss begins with the hours.

Twelve-hour days at the factory turn into eight hours and then six. I begin finding Papi home in the evenings, and after some weeks, I stop asking what happened, because all he says is, "*Se terminó el trabajo.*" The work came to an end, as if it were a line in a poem.

In the basement, he marks job listings in the Spanish newspaper in red ink with circles and *x*'s. At the unemployment agency, he sits alongside Pakistanis, Dominicans, and Nigerians, and he comes home to us with the English words for the work he does: embroidery worker, machine operator.

Factories begin closing for a week, a month, and we wait for the phone to ring. The calls come randomly. At first, the voices are pure American English. It is a language that rarely falters, that enjoys the certainty of punctuation marks. It begins with a "Hey, your dad home?" and ends with a casual "Thanks."

I am never to say that my father is out looking for another job or that he's found a part-time one. I am never to reveal anything on the phone. Just take the message and translate it into Spanish.

Sometimes, the factory has not closed, but they call to say: "Tell your dad to come at eight, not five." "Tell him we need him tonight." "Tell him to call next week." "Tell him he can file for unemployment."

The factories change hands. The American voices are replaced by those of immigrants, by an English that has learned the significance of proper names, verbs, and dates but not of conjunctions or prepositions. "Ygnacio?" they demand.

"He's not home."

"Tell him: No work, come Friday."

Men's factories lay off workers, but the ones for women keep them without pay. Sometimes, three weeks go by without a paycheck. Some women leave, but new ones show up, desperate to take a chance.

Sometimes on a Friday, the forelady announces she will have paychecks.

The women punch the clock and race each other to the bank. The ones who arrive last, like my mother, find a teller saying, "There's not enough funds to cash this check."

The women who have cars, used Toyotas, used Hondas, the women who have boyfriends with these cars, are the lucky ones. They reach the bank first and drive home with their pay: a hundred and eighty dollars for forty hours of work.

The dreaded question comes on Wednesday afternoon when my father drags the trash can to the curb. That's when the Colombian lady from across the street spots him. She asks about his job and when he tells her the factory is closed *por ahora*, she tilts her head like she already knew. "*Y estás colectando?*"

She has noticed my father at home lately and what she really wants to know is if he's collecting unemployment benefits.

"There's no work to be found," my father answers. His pants are falling from his narrow hips and he yanks them up with his left hand.

"*Pero, estás colectando?*"

My father shrugs his shoulders. "*Es la misma basura.*" It's the same garbage.

He wishes the Colombian lady well. From my bedroom window, I watch him walk into the house. In the basement, he finishes a six-pack of Coors beer and listens to Radio Wado. He's found a store on Bergenline Avenue where the price of beer seems to drop every time unemployment rises.

While my father and Mami and Tía Chuchi begin to collect unemployment, I am in high school, learning from school teachers and textbooks that Americans are trying to keep up with a family named the Joneses. These Joneses are a mystery of the English language, a fictional family that inspires anxiety in grown men who drive American cars and work in office buildings. My mother, however, has never heard of La Familia Yoneses, and if I told her about them, she would tell me to quit worrying about what everyone else is doing and focus on my own self.

In our part of the world, no one is keeping up.

We belong to a community based in part on the fact that we are all doing somewhat badly. When someone does a little better, there is an unspoken betrayal. We force a smile at them and murmur how good it is that they have a new job or are going to Puerto Rico for a visit. When they leave, we talk about how they are lying for their welfare checks, working *por la izquierda*, putting on airs. When we are the ones doing better, the women snack on *arepas* and complain, "It's incredible, but it's true. Any little good thing you got, somebody else wants."

In our own kitchen, we discuss *la envidia*, how envious people can be, how it is a sickness that eats away at a person. We make the sign of the cross and thank God for not making us too *ambiciosas*. It is a comforting ritual to talk like this. It keeps us from admitting that people have a right to want something better. It keeps us from thinking that we want something better.

It takes years for me to understand that the Joneses happen in houses where people cook in one room and eat in another. The Joneses do not happen in places where people are called white trash and spics, welfare queens and illegals, and no one asks the Joneses if they are collecting.

Spanish is a Romance language, except when you are trying to make ends meet.

The Spanish we share at home is a language where life is reduced to saying what you need, what's working, and what isn't. *No hay trabajo. Media libra de chuletas. Van pa' la iglesia. Estás colectando?*

Are you collecting?

The rest of that sentence, the words "unemployment benefits," does not crossover into Spanish. There is no need for translation because everyone here knows what is meant when the question is asked. No one says we are entitled to the money, because no one here believes we have such rights.

I come home to find my mother watching a telenovela. "Your father's in the basement," she says. "They called from work, said to not come today."

In the basement, my father talks with Elegguá. When he's collecting unemployment, he feeds the orisha more chocolates and Cuban coffee so the god will open the door to another job. My Elegguá is in the writing. Everyone tells me so at the barbecues for my mother's and sister's birthdays. "Girl, you're going to be something someday. You're going to make it. Amparo, look at this thing the girl wrote for the school paper, her name and everything."

No one ever says where I am going, but they are sure that a place is waiting for me. By the time I am nine years old and translating my report card for my father, I know he is not going with me.

There are many stages of development for a child who translates.

First, you are brought out among family and friends like a much-anticipated Christmas present and told to recite nursery rhymes from school. No one understands what you're saying, but everyone smiles, cheers, applauds.

Next, you are trusted to interpret on the bus, at the dentist, before schoolteachers. You stumble over verbs, insert nouns from the other language, hope you got enough of the information correct.

Then, you are called to answer the phone, because it's the electric company or the cable company or the Italian running for mayor again, and your father grumbles, "*Yo no sé lo que dice,*" or your mother calls out in alarm: "*Ven, que es en inglés!*"

Finally, after years of interpretation, you are trusted with paper. The final act: translation.

I am assigned to read and fill out my father's unemployment papers. Pen in hand, I sit at the kitchen table, terrorized. One false move, an error in my understanding between English and Spanish, could result in what I can only imagine as devastation: the absence of those checks in the mailbox.

Positioning myself stiffly in the seat as my high school teachers do when they are about to administer a test, I ask my father the cold, bitter questions:

> Have you had the chance for employment in the past week?
>
> Have you had offers of employment that you've turned down?
>
> Have you worked during the weeks for which you are claiming?

We repeat this exercise, my father and I, over the years. By the time I am in college, it is routine. I don't ask the questions. I run my pen down the unemployment form, checking off the answers while munching on dry cereal. Then, I drop my father off at the unemployment agency in Englewood on my way to a college class on microeconomics.

Sometimes, as my father walks away from the car, I linger. I consider if I should skip class and accompany him. I wonder if he will make it through with the English he knows. I worry that he'll be assigned to an unforgiving woman at the agency. There's always one, sometimes more, women with dull eyes and no patience, no Spanish.

But I drive away. It is what my father expects of me, what we all expect of me. I am to avoid manual labor, to graduate from college, to work with white people, to earn enough money to buy a house in a white neighborhood. I am to be one of those people who say they are of Hispanic heritage, who say they grew up in difficult circumstances, who see the assimilation of one person as the progress of a community.

My father and I—we are not *uña y mugre*—but we have no way of knowing that my lingering outside of the unemployment agency, my thought of going in, of speaking up, might signal that I am on a road neither one of us has seen before.

My father always comes home to my mother.

He arrives with bloody hands. Sometimes it is because of a simple cut. Sometimes because he stubbed his thumb with a hammer. He is probably not fit for work as a handyman, but it pays. And it sends him home needing my mother. Wanting her.

On a Sunday evening, after dinner, after my mother has washed the dishes, my father sits at the kitchen table and opens his hands, palm up.

My mother examines the skin and squints. "There it is. I see it."

"A splinter?" he asks.

She nods and saturates a cotton ball with rubbing alcohol. Holding his hand in hers, she wipes the skin with the moist white cotton. Then, she examines a small stuffed animal that's punctured with sewing needles. She chooses a needle and wipes it with alcohol. Her head bent over the wounded hand, she slowly begins pushing the needle into the thick skin, the metal tip nudging the threadlike piece of wood, coaxing it from its sanctuary.

My father stares out the kitchen window where his black jeans hang on the laundry line, a stone expression on his face. A few times, he winces.

When someone asks my father how he is doing, he looks at his hands, studies the scattering of scars and the dryness of skin. His answer is always the same, *"Ahí caballero, en la misma lucha."*

When I ask him what it means to say you are in the same *lucha,* my father says it means you are doing the same old thing.

Years later, surrounded by feminists, by activists, by artists, I hear that word again: we're in this *lucha* together. The word means struggle, someone tells me. The same old thing, the struggle, *la lucha.*

I sit in an organizing meeting, my hand clasping a pen. It's hard to explain how someone translates a word and your understanding of your family and your history and everything that's come before turns around, opens to interpretation.

In the nineties, the unemployment agency sends a notice: we need to call in to a new dial-in system to collect. The brochure comes in Spanish and English.

My mother studies it carefully. My father's hands can do many things but handling money is not one of them. Making phone calls is not one of them. It is my mother who writes the checks, pays the bills, and besieges me when it's time to fill out the unemployment forms. It is she who calls in to the new dial-in system.

My father's hands shake me until I wake up in the bottom bunk. It is early morning and he is still sober. "Your mother called unemployment and couldn't get through. Come on, get up, call them."

The dial-in system is efficient. Much more so than the factories that closed.

If your Social Security number ends in an odd number, call on Tuesday.

If it's an even number, call on Thursday.

Enter the weeks for which you are claiming.

The dial-in system is clever. The brochure insists it is to help us avoid waiting at the agency, but it is also the best way to handle the possibility of riots as the economy switches from manufacturing to service jobs. Not making a trip to the agency means we don't have to see in one room how many other people are going through the same experience. When we do show up (because the phone system is down), the number of people is fewer, even though back on our street we know there are more people out of work. Still, we begin to doubt ourselves. Maybe it isn't so bad.

Not going to the unemployment agency means we can avoid seeing the pain of other people. We don't need to know English to understand the black security guard telling someone on the line, "No, sir. According to this, you have nothing left to collect." We don't need a translation for the immigrant man's English words, "But I no find job." And then that dreaded English word: welfare.

"Sir, I'm gonna need for you to get off this line because we can't help you here. Get on the line at window four and you can talk to someone there about welfare."

Calling in now for unemployment, we can avoid that man's eyes, the way his brown body sheltered under layers of clothes against the winter storm does not go to window four. He turns away and leaves through the front door. And we wonder where he is headed with those empty hands.

Not going to the unemployment agency, we can avoid thinking about what will happen when none of us can collect any longer.

—ᴍ—

The newspapers and books and the six o'clock news don't, in those years, say that grown men and women are losing their jobs, that Washington has agreed to let the corporations travel without visas, that people are sifting through the debris after the storm. That will come later. For now, they use short hand: NAFTA.

My father finds new work. He washes floors and dishes at the Meadowlands Sports Complex. He is sixty-three. The dark curls have vanished and the hairline has receded, leaving a thin line of gray hair at the back of his head.

Service work is different from factory labor. It is not only the absence of the large machines or the union benefits. It's the distance from home. The two buses needed to reach the job. It is the bitterness that slips into the voice, that makes my father snap at me one day, "You're not the one cleaning up after people every night."

Sometimes on weekends, I wake up in the dark, dress silently, and drive my father to work despite his protests, his arguments that I sleep longer. He believes I need more rest. "*Gastas la cabeza,*" he says about my job in book publishing.

In those early hours of the morning, the Meadowlands Sports Complex reminds me of the Vatican, a series of gray buildings that thrust out from the land like fists into the air. I am not allowed inside the sports complex. There are identification cards, security guards.

"Leave me here," my father barks when we reach the main entrance.

I watch him walk toward that fist of a building, his thin body in dark jeans and boots, a flannel jacket and baseball cap protecting him from the wind. It is in those moments that I doubt myself, that I wonder if arranging words on a computer screen and sharing them with others makes any difference, if that is the best I can do with my own hands.

It will take years to understand that writing makes everything else possible. Writing is how I learn to love my father and where I come from. Writing is how I leave him and also how I take him with me.

In a darkroom in Manhattan, I wait.

For the last two weeks, I have been studying photography on weekends. I have learned that taking pictures is about how light enters the world. It is about the speed at which I allow that light to arrive on the page, the choices I make about what to include in the frame.

We wait now with the chemicals and muted light bulbs. My teacher is showing us how to slip the paper into the bins of chemical mixtures, how to move the paper once it is submerged, how to be ready for the arrival of an image. I stare at the sheet I have placed in the bin, my eyes alert. My father is in the paper.

His hands rise to the surface slowly as dark spots emerging from the light. Little by little, one hand comes into view. It's in his lap; the other is holding a can of beer. He is shirtless at the kitchen table. What the picture did not record is that he had examined his hands, called me over, told me I should photograph this one scar on his index finger. He couldn't remember how it had happened

The photograph is blurry.

In the darkroom, the teacher, an older black man, peers over my shoulder. He gives me technical advice for next time, pointers on shutter speeds, lighting, the frame. He examines the photograph again.

"Your father?" he asks.

"Yes."

A pause.

"He has character," the teacher says quietly before moving on to the next student.

Blackout

I didn't think white people got jobs the way Latinos did, just by talking to each other. But they do, and that's how it happens for me. My first big job as a writer.

It's the end of a graduate journalism class at New York University. The room fills with the familiar cacophony of a class ending: chairs scraping floors, students unzipping bags, murmurs about lunch and papers due. The professor, a thin, white woman, fastens her eyes on me.

"An editor at the *New York Times* is looking for a researcher for a book she's doing on women's history," she says, matter-of-fact. "I thought of you. You write about feminism."

I smile politely, uncomfortably. I'm twenty-five and writing for *Ms.* magazine, but I don't consider myself someone who writes about feminism. That sounds like work other people do, people who are rich or famous or smart. I'm not a *boba* though. I have spent enough time around white women to know it's better to not argue with them.

When I meet the editor, I like her immediately. She's unpretentious and direct but warm in that "do you want water or tea" sort of way. I have no idea that she's the first woman to run the editorial page at the newspaper. What I do know is that Gail is going to be the first (and only) lady who pays me money to track down what indigenous women used as menstrual pads back in the pre-tampon days. That's my first assignment, and I set off, gathering phone numbers for anthropologists and historians, generating a spreadsheet to track my interviews and library reading, and returning with my final report. (They used rags, the natural kind.)

Months later, I e-mail Gail an opinion piece I wrote for an online wire service and she shoots back: "*Oye*, you should apply for this internship here in the editorial department."

She doesn't write "*oye*," but she might as well have, because the way she e-mails with such ease is how a woman on the bus tells my mother, "*Oye*, there's this factory down on Hudson Avenue that's hiring."

Oye, and just like that I send my resume, which now includes research on indigenous maxi pads, to the editor at the *Times* hiring interns, even though I have no idea what an editorial is. That's right. I am twenty-five, I am writing for a national magazine, I have been in journalism school, and I do not know what an editorial is.

I want to say that it's never come up, that no one has ever talked to me about editorials. But they probably did, and I didn't know what it was, and as I've been doing since I was in kindergarten, I probably acted like I knew what they were talking about and promptly forgot it.

Now I walk around the block to the Greek deli. I pass the women and men waiting at the bus stop, buy a copy of the *Times* and flip over the A section. A friend has told me to look at the left side of the last page, at the short paragraphs stacked like shoe boxes in a closet.

The writing carries no byline. It's monotonous, and I realize why I don't know what an editorial is. I've never made it past the second line.

My feelings, though, are irrelevant. This is the *New York Times*. They have Maureen Dowd and stringers all over the world, including countries I have to find in the *Britannica* encyclopedia. If I get the internship, they won't actually let me write.

But they do.

—∿—

My summer internship begins on the tenth floor of the *New York Times* building on Forty-Third Street. The first days are heady: the large, revolving doors at the main entrance, the elevator racing upward, a massive desk of my own, the thick, solid wooden shelves in the library filled with old books and newspapers and magazines. It's nine months since September 11, and Howell Raines is the executive editor. He supposedly has a penchant for the visual, which is why, a staff reporter tells me, the corridors are now filled with large-scale reproductions of photographs that have been in the paper. My favorite ones, the ones that make me pause, are the aerial photographs of New York City, the tops of skyscrapers like the closed beaks of birds.

I'm taken to lunch that week, shown how the computer system works, told to wait a minute while an editor, a white man with sharp eyes, answers a call and laughs about how India and Pakistan need to get it together and play nice. I'm told how to put editorials in a queue, how to see what other people are writing for the next day or the weekend edition, how to answer my editor's questions online. I'm told to join the editorial board for their meetings in the morning.

The meetings take place in a conference room. Inside are a long wooden table, large heavy chairs, and a television in a cabinet. Men show up in stiff white shirts with cups of coffee in hand, notepads and pens, and the day's paper. The women show up in slacks and button-down shirts with notepads and pens and the paper. They file in one by one, welcome me, make jokes about this and that, and it begins to dawn on me that they are regular white people.

I'm not sure what I expected them to look like, but I figured that writing for the *New York Times* would turn a person into something close to God, or at least Oprah Winfrey. I expected that they would look different somehow, more beautiful, more pristine, that they wouldn't have to read the day's paper because they would have a secret telephone they could pick up and hear about what was happening in the world.

What's not surprising is that they are white.

It's about a dozen people, and they're all white except for one black man and one man who is white (blond actually) but Mexican. I sit at the table, terrified that I'll say something stupid and more terrified that I won't be able to say anything at all.

The meetings begin, and they go around the table, pitching ideas, shooting down ideas, bantering. A writer with a head full of white hair, a man who could be a grandpa on an after-school TV special, says, "Now I have an idea you're not going to like . . ." and everyone grins. There's much about which to have opinions—the war on terror, Bush, stem-cell research—but this man wants to write about the Superfund sites everyone else wants to forget.

Assignments are made. One writer sighs. "Yes, I guess I'm the one to do it," he says. Then they retreat to their offices to make phone calls, conduct interviews, and write opinions.

My first idea for an editorial is straightforward, a no-brainer really. I think the *New York Times* editorial board should urge President Bush to grant Colombians political asylum in the United States. The issue is clear: the United States funds the war in Colombia and the people deserve relief.

To back up my idea I start making phone calls, and I quickly learn that people will talk to me. The name *New York Times*, in fact, produces the most spectacular effects on people. Local advocates return my calls with eager voices. Government spokespeople chat me up with fake grins. A number of people bristle at the name; others ask to have lunch with me. Me. An intern.

By the time I call an advocate at Human Rights Watch that summer about another topic, I am covered in arrogance. I announce that I'm phoning from the *Times*, but when I pause for effect, the woman snaps, "Which *Times?*"

I bite my lip, sure this woman has, with female intuition alone, figured out that I'm only a summer intern. "The *New York Times,*" I answer, doing my best to control the pitch of my voice.

"If you don't say that, I can't possibly know," the woman answers, adding that there is the *Los Angeles Times* and *Time* magazine. But I hear it in her voice. The nervous laugh. The slight faltering, the retreating.

The paper, I begin to learn that summer, is not a series of pages bound together. It's not even the people themselves, the ones sitting at the conference table three times a week or the ones reporting the news. It's something else. It's an idea that produces tension in people or arouses their flattery. It has the power to agitate. It's kind of like God, but not in the way I expected. It doesn't feel good.

The other discovery I make is about white people.

One of the editors, a skinny man who I'll call Mr. Flaco, listens to my initial idea for an editorial about granting Colombians asylum. "Why Colombians and not another group of people?" he asks, patronizingly. "If you open the door for them, do you open the door to every other country with internal conflicts?"

Mr. Flaco's questions are rational, but they also feel odd somehow. When I board the bus for Jersey, I'm still thinking about what he asked.

In Jersey, I step off the bus a few feet from the Greek deli and Chinese restaurant. The street is littered with candy wrappers, the trash bin filled to capacity with soda cans. I walk past the long line at the bus stop, wondering who there is a Salvadoreño with political asylum and who is Honduran and Guatemalan and without *papeles*. They wear, all of them, jeans and jackets and baseball caps. They're waiting for the 165, the 166, transfer tickets and bus passes in hand.

Do you open the door to every other country with internal conflicts?

It's true that Colombians are not the only ones in need of asylum. It is every group from practically every country where the United States and Europe have at some point staked a claim on land. From the perspective of here, which is to say from the perspective of the United States, of this skinny editor, of people who have power, Colombia is not as devastated as Rwanda or even as El Salvador was in the eighties. Colombians are suffering, yes, but not as much.

There is a hierarchy of pain, and it is no longer confined to the pages of my college textbooks about political theory. It is here in Mr. Flaco. Pain in and of itself is not enough. It matters how many are dead, how many wounded, over what period of time, how much public outrage there is in the West. The pain has to be significant in relationship to those in power. By contrast, we (my family and the men at the bus stop and me) are free to make demands, to share outrage, to know solidarity.

Realizing this does not depress me. I consider it a discovery, because it feels that way, like I have entered the collective mind of white people with political power everywhere and managed to see one of the strange rituals by which they reproduce. This, I can only imagine, is how Darwin must have felt.

Because it's the beginning of summer, NPR has an obligatory story about the high number of girls who are going to tanning salons. I listen to this while lying in bed next to my girlfriend, who frequents these salons, and with my idea for getting Colombians political asylum stalled, I suggest writing on the evils of the fake tan.

Mr. Flaco loves it. White men can always be counted on to agree that girls do crazy things in the name of beauty and that they need to be chastised. Who better than to scold teenage girls than a young woman herself?

I put these thoughts aside and sit at my computer monitor in my office on the tenth floor writing the best opinion piece I can muster. Although the topic is one that slightly depresses me (I could be writing about the impact of the civil war in Colombia!), I nevertheless find myself humming and tapping away at the keyboard, having the experience that comes whenever I write: a rush of joy through my body. I feel energized, happy, strong, even.

At the end of the day, I get on the elevator exhausted, my face slightly flushed. I am living a life I could never have imagined, even if it is about suntans.

At the *Times*, people spend their days writing and then get paid every two weeks. It happens even if you disagree with Mr. Flaco or if you write a bad piece that needs tons of editing. You still get paid.

So, convinced that this life can't be mine, I insist on taking my intern paycheck to the bank every two weeks and cashing it. Each time the black teller hands me the stack of hundred dollar bills, I feel that I am real and that this is really happening to me.

It is a lesson I learned from my mother.

On Fridays, if she had been paid at the factory, Tía Chuchi would take my sister and me to meet my mother at the bank, where she would be waiting on line with a check, that precious slip of paper in her hand. She would take the money from the bank teller in one swift move, as if someone was going to steal it from her, and then she would move over to the side and count the bills, slipping them into a small envelope the way she would place a pillow in a pillowcase. Those dollars were freedom. We could afford an evening meal at McDonald's and *pasteles*, too.

Several times a month, people visit the editorial board. Sometimes they are invited; sometimes they have lobbied to meet with the writers. Sometimes it's people's chance to talk about their issues; sometimes it's the board members who have asked to hear someone's perspective.

Cookies and coffee are served, and we show up with notepads and pens. If it is an extremely important person, like the head of the FBI or a superstar academic who wrote a new book about the economy, lunch is served.

It is during one of these visits that I find myself meeting Mr. Alvaro Uribe.

For months now, my mother's kitchen has been plagued with his name. Colombians in Jersey and Queens and Florida were able to vote for him in the presidential election, and my aunties have been anxious. Will Mr. Uribe be able to do anything, however small, to end the civil war that's held Colombia hostage since the sixties? The answer, of course, is no. It takes a movement, not a lone man, but people being people and aunties being aunties, they fantasize about being rescued.

Mr. Uribe comes from a wealthy family and he's promising to be Colombia's Rudy Giuliani. He is vowing law and order in a country known for drug cartels, magical realism, and the kidnapping of gringos. His own father was killed by the so-called rebel groups who are now drug trafficking, and Mr. Uribe is rumored to have ties to the paramilitaries, the privately funded armies who massacre civilians.

But in the editorial conference room on the tenth floor, Mr. Uribe hardly looks like someone privy to murders. He could be one of my uncles, a short man stuffed into a suit and not permitted, for the moment, to drink whiskey or curse in front of company. He proclaims that the coffee is not very good and then he makes a little speech about his Giuliani-style plan and takes questions. It dawns on me that he is here, because he has to be, like when my mother and tías would force me to leave the books in my bedroom and meet their friends for coffee.

"Many Colombians in the States are hoping for temporary protection status," I say. "Will you take up that issue?"

His lips curve into a small sneer. "They voted for me, so I have to ask for it."

Later in the day, it occurs to me that for the first time I met someone who may be responsible for the murders of many people, and I asked him a polite question.

—〰—

It is a custom in Latino families like mine that you live at home until you marry. Even if you go away for college, which I didn't, you still come home when you graduate.

I have already broken this rule once, going to live with a boyfriend at nineteen. But the moment the relationship soured, about a year later, I returned home. Now at twenty-seven, I am ready to leave. This time permanently. I just have to deliver the news.

In the kitchen, my parents and Tía Chuchi are watching the *noticias*. It is evening and everyone is done with dinner. My father is drinking his beer. The window shades are drawn, but the voices of children playing in yards and on the streets below come up in bursts of firecrackers.

"I'm going to live in the city," I announce.

Everyone turns their head toward me. No one speaks. Then my father looks back at the television, and my mother and auntie do the same. I wait for some questions but they don't come. Not then. They arrive the next day and the day after: Is it a safe place? Are you sure? You'll be closer to work, yes, but . . .

They want to argue with me, but they can't. I have married the best man I could possibly find—the *New York Times*—and we all know it.

My mother and Tía Chuchi go with me to buy spoons and forks, a Brita water filter, and curtains with a flower pattern. They help me set up the apartment, an illegal studio on the Upper East Side that's about the size of the bedroom I shared with my sister. When they leave, I am left with myself in a way that feels new. I am on my own for the first time in my life. *My very own place.* I have the sensation of having escaped a burning building. I have a job. A good job. And my own illegal sublet. I am paying my rent and groceries and not doing it by working at a factory or cleaning toilets.

The New York Times building has windows like a cathedral's: tall, large, indulgent with how much sunlight they permit indoors. I walk up to the fourteenth floor one afternoon and stare out a closed window, mesmerized that Manhattan can actually be reduced to a miniature city, that the millions of feet and voices cannot be seen or heard from here but are nevertheless in perpetual motion.

I love the quiet here, the space to contemplate how quickly perspective can be changed, to wonder how a man like Uribe, who loses his father, makes peace with grief or doesn't, to think about what a man on the editorial board said to me: "I bet no one else has written for this editorial page whose parents didn't speak English."

In a few weeks' time it will be the first anniversary of September 11 and with it will come the rush of memory, of women and men who—hundreds of feet above the city—stepped into the sky that morning to escape the heat and the twisting metal and the violence of not choosing their last moments.

But before the anniversary, about two weeks before, a white man from the *Times*, a business editor, will look out a window like this one. He will be up one more flight of stairs and maybe he will wonder about the sky and the city and perspective. Or maybe not. The pain by then will be squeezing at him too much. He will prop open the window, place his face to the city air, and step into the sky.

Mr. Flaco is curious to hear what I might want to write about a new report showing that boys are being left behind in education. Nervous, I stumble through my pitch about how it's not all boys. It is black boys and teenagers. "Racism," I begin, "has, you know, shaped the expectations the kids have of themselves and that teachers have of them."

"What's going to be your recommendation?" he asks, a smile dancing at his lips. "Tell teachers to raise their self-esteem?"

I stare at the carpet. He continues. "What's remarkable is that when you look across socioeconomic levels, black boys consistently do badly in school. It doesn't matter if they're living in Westchester or Harlem."

The air around me grows thin, choking.

"By comparison," he says, "Chinese kids do well in school even when they just got here yesterday." He chuckles. "It's like it's genetic."

I glance at him to make sure he is really here in the room with me, that he has actually said those words. I don't expect to see the familiar face of the skinny man I have known for two months. Surely his words have distorted his forehead and his eyelids and his nostrils. But no such thing has happened. He is still the same man with the *flaco* face and a high-up job at an important institution. A Mr. Uribe. He grins at me, like we're best friends.

In Times Square, the taxis blare, the trucks screech, the tourists squeal and position themselves for photos. It's August and the air is thick with humidity and the grease of hotdogs being sold by street vendors. The tourists point their cameras at each other and then up at the billboards. They have come from all parts of the country and the world to be here under these towering ads and bright lights, and as I watch them I begin to consider that maybe I don't want to be here.

It's not because of Mr. Flaco the Racist. Or Mr. Uribe the Killer. I don't know what it is. The streets vibrate with too many people, and the billboards tower over us with white faces, white teeth, white summer cotton, and I find that I don't have the words. As much as I want to leave, I can't.

This is my big opportunity, the moment I have been preparing for my whole life. People like me, from the community I come from, we don't just get to work at the *New York Times*. Rosa Parks sat down, Martin Luther King Jr. stood up, and my parents paid for Catholic high school so I could be here. Whatever I do, I can't say no. I have to say yes, yes, and yes again.

When Gail asks if I want to pursue this journalism business, I say yes, and I find myself with a year-long internship on the third floor reporting for the metro desk.

Newsrooms are set up like mazes.

It is an endless series of desks and television screens, and everywhere you turn is another white man. You are meant to be the intern who gets lost and can't find the elevators, or at least I am. Looking out across the third floor, I see only receding hairlines, white foreheads, and bushy eyebrows. Somewhere in that I am supposed to find an editor with a name like Bob or Jennifer. Locating my new desk—amid the clacking of keyboards and droning of television news—becomes my accomplishment that first week.

It doesn't take long, though, to see that I am missing a crucial asset: a talent for talking to white men.

I have a good deal of experience with white women. I learned their mannerisms right alongside lessons in English, algebra, and chemistry. If I count my entire schooling starting with kindergarten, that is nineteen years of studying white women. It is easy, then, to now make small talk with them. I nod sympathetically about children, inquire about their favorite movies, commiserate about the morning commute.

But white men are different.

After two weeks in the newsroom, I see that talking to white men boils down to a crude combination of cracking jokes about children and the morning commute, referring to sports teams and events at random, and imparting snide comments about this book or that article. It is especially impressive if you can comment on something buried deep in a news story, since everyone knows that no one actually reads the story to the end. Talking to white men, then, has a pattern, a set of rules, but try as I might, I can't learn them. My mind blanks when they joke with me. I find myself nodding and looking the other way, hoping they will leave me alone.

What's worse is that I have absolutely no instinct for reporting. None.

"Here's the news release," an editor tells me. "I need copy by three."

I nod, sit at my computer, and look at the paper. Something about a food-borne illness. I stare at the words and wonder what I'm supposed to do.

Writing an opinion, even a stiff editorial, comes easily to me. My mind immediately reaches for questions, important points, people to interview. But reporting produces in me a condition akin to stage fright. My body freezes, my mind stares at a blank white wall. Even though I'm doing exactly what I would do in the editorial department, here in the newsroom, without the option of forming an opinion, I have to remind myself of what to do: make calls, ask questions, quote, summarize, send to editor, wait.

After that first story, editors send me to get quotes from people on the street about an increase in subway fares. Then to interview people on the street about the mayor's new idea to ban loud noises. Then to take the subway to Brooklyn, because a fire there has killed a black child. Then to a Latino event to get the governor's reaction. Eight hours become ten, eleven, twelve. The copy editors call at seven, eight, and nine at night.

In the morning, I board the subway, exhausted. I spot that day's paper in someone's hands. A small thrill comes into my heart. Someone is about to read one of my stories. But the woman scans the headlines, flips the pages, and then folds the paper and stores it in her bag.

That's it. Twelve hours of work—by hundreds of reporters, stringers, editors, copy editors, designers, and deliverymen—were considered for a total of five seconds by a white woman on the Number 6 train. I meet humility for the first time, and I hate it.

One of the other young reporters decides that we need to meet with veterans at the paper for informal conversations about the business. This is her code for "I'm trying to move up," and the rest of us agree that it's a good idea. Someone from the powers-that-be says we can meet on the fourteenth floor, where the big private events happen.

I arrive early. I want to enjoy the quiet here, the cathedral windows, the sense that the city and even the newsroom, with its ringing phones and chatty television screens, are at a distance.

The veteran reporter steps into the room. He's an older man with a kind voice and gentle smile. We exchange a hello, but then his eyebrows furrow. He's staring at a door off to the side of the room. "Is the stairwell through there?" he asks.

"I think so."

He's lost now in his own world as he walks over and props the door open. I follow him. In the stairwell, he pauses at one of the windows, mentions the editor, the white man who killed himself, and grows silent.

The window pane here is dusty and *viejo*. It's late in the afternoon, and the light bathes the parapets of the building and even, I suppose, the place where the man met his final moment. The older reporter stares out the window, then inspects the frame and sighs deeply, and I begin to understand that I believed the TV shows I watched as a child. I believed bad things didn't happen to white people, not in places like this. But now here is the window, the man grieving, the light golden and punishing.

While I'm reporting for the *Times*, my father is spending his days in the basement where he's made a room of his own, apart from my mother and tías. He has his beer, his radio, even a mattress so he can take naps. He has set up a shower for himself.

I am afraid of finding him dead in the basement one day. Already once, he drank too much, fell, and cut his head open, and we had to rush him to the emergency room. But there is no use trying to get him out of the basement. It is a blessing that he lets me take him now for a visit to the doctor.

The waiting room is large enough for about fifty people, but it doesn't have a television, so everyone looks bored and restless. Papi is dressed in dark jeans, construction boots, and a flannel button-down shirt over a white Hanes T-shirt. He asks me about the *New York Times*, and I confide that I'm not liking it. He stares at the floor and says nothing.

Inside, he sits on the examination table, and I take the chair reserved for spouses or parents. I figure my father won't say anything about what I shared, but then without my prompting, he comments, "*Tú piensas que a mí me gusta mi trabajo? A mí no me gusta mi trabajo. A tu mamá tampoco.*"

That is what I record in my journal that night: "Do you think I like my work? I don't like my work. Your mother doesn't like hers either."

When the doctor arrives, I begin moving back and forth between Spanish and English admonishments: stop drinking, stop smoking, eat more vegetables, more fruits, more oranges.

"Oranges?" my father exclaims in Spanish. "No. That's all I ate in Cuba, only oranges. No oranges."

The doctor and I look at each other. After so many years of working in our community, he knows, like I do, that there is no use in arguing against memory.

Nor do I disagree with my father about whether or not people should have work they enjoy. But the next morning, I notice I have a hard time getting out of bed. Not an impossible time. Just a heaviness about me, as if the air itself were an open hand holding me down.

It's a cool night in November and I am walking on the Upper East Side, past doormen and women in three-inch heels hailing cabs and men in their fifties walking dogs the size of their briefcases. I am, as usual, lost in my inner world. I am contemplating a conversation or rewriting an article or wondering about the origin of three-inch heels. I am acutely aware of the streets in

Manhattan, of the way darkness never wins here, not even at night, but is always kept at bay by street lamps and the bobbing headlights of taxis and limos and buses. The city is a blitz of lights and sounds and smells, but I have learned to shut it out, to be in my own quiet place.

Tonight, however, is different.

I turn a corner, and the city yanks me from my inner world. Fifty feet up in the air is Kermit the Frog, his belly nearly touching the top of the street lamps, his fingers reaching to tap the windows of high rise buildings, his inflated balloon body covering a chunk of the Manhattan street.

It's the night before Thanksgiving Day, and the balloons are being prepared for their annual walk in the Macy's parade. It's the sort of the thing that can only happen in New York, not the balloons but finding their giant faces and hands around the corner, the way they make even this city feel small, insignificant. It feels magical and bizarre too, how the world can contain all of this, the plastic green frog, the memories and the oranges, the dead white man.

Editors were invented for several reasons, one of which is to torture interns.

It's a metro editor who decides that interns will spend time on the police beat helping to cover New York City's homicides, rapes, and robberies. The work mostly involves chatting with white police officers in charge of information they won't give you unless the two of you get along and they consider you something of a person they'd want to have a beer with. To say that I'm terrible at this would be putting it kindly.

The rest of the work, at least for me, involves watching a veteran reporter with reddish curls call the families of crime victims and say in a mournful tone, "I'm sorry for your loss. I was wondering if I could ask you a few questions."

The first few times, I stare at him, and when it's no longer polite to do so, I pretend to read online while listening to him. He sounds genuine and compassionate during every phone call. He modulates the tone of his voice, and I note how his English is comforting, the way a hand-rolled cigar feels, as if the earth has been gathered up, made compact, held steady. His voice reaches out to the other person, yes, but it also allows for mutual silence and then directs back to the questions, the information that's needed, the interview.

Then, the call is over, the moment has passed, and he's on to other calls, detectives, cops, higher-ups, and he's issuing orders, because another paper caught a piece of information we should have, and I'm off to the Bronx for a story about a young man named Buddha.

The hierarchy of pain has nuances.

The fact that Buddha murdered someone is news, because the victim was a child. If the child had been a few years older, if he had been not a child but instead a young black man, the editor would have said, "Victim and perp knew each other," which is the preferred way to explain that black men killing each other in the Bronx is not news.

But Buddha murdered a child, and he did so three days after Christmas, on a day when the news was slow.

He's in jail now, Buddha. It's his mother we are after. Me and reporters and stringers for local newspapers. I interview the neighbors and note the holiday decorations ("Peace and Joy"). Later, the district attorney's office will say that Buddha got his name because he was tall and fat, and that three days after Christmas, Buddha was bruised, not on his body but somewhere else. His heart or his ego. Another man, another tall, overweight black man had teased Buddha. Words were thrust back and forth between them, threatened to erupt into fists, into gunshots, but the women stepped in. The *novias*. And the air became if not calm, then, at least, still. Buddha and the man parted ways.

But Buddha followed him, not the man, but the man's little cousin, thirteen-year-old Brandon. In an elevator, Buddha towered over the youngster, and while boasting of how he planned to hurt the other man, his mirror image, Buddha shoved Brandon against the wall of the elevator and shot him in the head.

The elevator reached the twelfth floor. It was after midnight. The door must have opened then, mechanically, indifferently, and spilt the boy's blood.

Now the elevator door creaks open and Buddha's mother steps into the narrow hallway. She's pushing a shopping cart. It has two six packs of beer. She refuses, however, to talk to us as she opens the door to her apartment. She's a heavy black woman with colorless eyes and deep lines set in her face, and my first thought is that no one is going to tell her story, the story of how she probably falls asleep at night in front of the television set with a can of beer still open, like my father, and how she raised a family here so many hundreds of feet above the Bronx, and how she bathed Buddha when he was an infant and fed him WIC baby formula and now all she wants to do is smack him.

There are also the other stories, the ones about how these neighborhoods were set up, how white men decided where black families would live, how it came to be that Buddha grew up in a place where you carry a gun to come and go from home and kill a boy who looks like a younger version of yourself.

I don't have words for these other stories, only the feeling of them inside of me like pebbles piled at the corner of a child's desk.

There were other black reporters in the newsroom at the *New York Times* besides Jayson Blair. When I think back to that time, though, to the spring of 2003, I can only see Jayson.

He is writing front-page stories for the paper about Iraq War veterans. I know he was once an intern like me, but what I haven't figured out yet is if he's quiet and withdrawn because he's brilliant or if something is wrong with him. The fact that he wears long sweaters instead of shirts and ties unsettles me. It isn't the sort of thing a white man would do here, let alone a young black man. I keep wanting to tuck his shirt in. I tease him once or twice about being short. He's polite, but it's clearly a sore point with him, and I leave him alone.

It turns out, though, that he has good reason to keep to himself. Jayson is drinking, lying, and plagiarizing his stories. Front-page stories.

"Did you hear?" another intern asks me.

I nod. "Crazy." I figure the paper will run an apology and move on.

But there isn't an apology. The story unravels. The anxieties of white people, the ones kept behind private doors, burst and the other newspapers report them: Jayson only got as far as he did because he's black. A fellow intern comes up to me, irritated. "Why are people thinking it's okay to say racist shit in front of me?"

She's holding a cup of coffee. We both glance across the newsroom, across the cubicles and the tops of people's heads. I have no way, none really, of knowing who in the room is a Mr. Flaco, and this is part of the agreement we make by working here, as people of color. We don't know who harbors doubts about our capacity to think and work and write. We don't know, not really, who we can trust.

Jayson, meanwhile, is rumored to be shut away in his apartment, and as a friend of mine puts it, the white people do then what they always do when they get nervous: they call a meeting.

The meeting is held on Forty-Fourth Street, in a theater. I get in line along with hundreds of reporters and administrative staff and editors. The executive editor and managing editor and publisher sit before us on a stage. They're going to explain what happened. Sort of.

There isn't an easy way to tell us that someone who was mentally unstable managed to get a job at the world's most recognized newspaper and snuck lies past more than one or two or even three editors. I sit in the audience and inspect my identification card. I don't like sports where a person is put in a ring to get beat up. Besides, no one is going to talk about race. Not in an honest way.

But I'm wrong.

The executive editor, Howell Raines, has the mic. He's from the South, he reminds us, a place where a man has to choose where he stands on race. "Does that mean I personally favored Jayson? Not consciously. But you have a right to ask if I, as a white man from Alabama with those convictions, gave him one chance too many. . . ."

I wince and I pray that he won't go there, because if he does it will not be cute. It will not be understood by the hundreds of white people in the theater. But he does it. He goes there.

Did he, as a white man from Alabama, give a young black man too many chances? "When I look into my own heart for the truth of that," he admits, "the answer is yes."

It's been eight years since that day in the theater, and I'm thinking again about a white man confessing to his own people that he cared about the black community, that he thought he could single-handedly change a hierarchy. I'm thinking about the whiteness of the news organization and how that whiteness reproduced itself with every hire, every promotion, but that is not a scandal.

He left, the editor. He was fired and the metro editor—a white man who once told me that community-based organizations, the ones helping poor people of color, were no longer rele-

vant—was hailed as a savior because he had tried to stop Jayson
from writing for the paper.

A week or so after the theater meeting, I meet the Jourdans.
   They are Haitians. They came to New York City one by one
over the course of thirty years: Patrick, Paul, Cosner. They knew
that life would be easier the closer they lived to white Americans.
They earned their money; they sent it back home. They brought
another brother, a sister and a young cousin. Together, some of
them with spouses, they shared the basement apartment and second floor of a two-story home in Brooklyn.
   They learned to have familial love by telephone calls. Like Tía
Chuchi, they probably bought the wallet-size phone cards and
used pennies to scratch the personal identification numbers. The
Jourdans probably called the 800 number and an automated
woman's voice asked them for the PIN and then told them how
much money they had to call Aquin, their home town, how much
time they had with the people they loved.
   Maybe that's what Cosner Jourdan did on Saturdays. He
walked the neighborhood most days. At sixty-six, he had diabetes
and had retired from factory work. He had been in Brooklyn for
ten years and he took care of two trees outside of his basement
apartment. He had friends, people who loved him.
   On the night of May 29, 2003, however, a fire breaks out
around three in the morning. It rips through the basement apartment. The smoke spreads to the other floors, and the brothers,
their spouses, sister, and young cousin flee to the streets. But not
Cosner. He dies in the basement from smoke inhalation.
   Because his death happens on a day when the news is slow,
the story catches my editor's attention, and I arrive at the Jourdan
house along with reporters from other papers. We all scribble the
pertinent facts: Cosner's age, the names of the brothers, the cause
of death. The other reporters leave the scene in a matter of

minutes having deduced that there is no news. I see the same thing, but I stay.

Perhaps it is the basement.

Layers of soot cover a bicycle and shopping cart. Hours after the fire, it's still hard to breathe in the basement. I sit with the Jourdan brothers on the front stoop as friends and neighbors come by. They speak in Creole about the night and Cosner's death. I ask a few questions from time to time, but mostly I watch the sadness on their faces.

The day is hot; sweat coats my back and drenches my button-down shirt. In his last moments, did Cosner dream of his father, of his homeland? Did he wake up and think it was his father's birthday that day, that the old man was turning ninety-eight and what would he say when he received the news? His son, dead.

Remembering now that day with the Jourdans, I think: we were not meant to be here. We were not meant to die underground engulfed in smoke. Not Cosner, not any of us. The death of a Haitian man is not some accident in the middle of the night, but that is how it is reported. It is how I reported it.

I wish I had saved my notes from that day, but I threw them out. I discarded them because it was perhaps that day sitting in the thick heat of a Brooklyn summer with the Jourdans that I began to feel a cracking inside of me.

I first read that word *cracking* in an F. Scott Fitzgerald essay called "The Crack-Up." I didn't know much about his writing, only that he had become a writer and earned a lot of money and did not live in basements. Everyone had told me as a child that I would be like Fitzgerald one day, without the booze and early death. I would do more with my life than work to pay the rent. I would write, and in writing, I would help people.

But sitting in Brooklyn, surrounded by the somber faces of Haitian men and the smell of soot, it begins to seem to me that things are not going to turn out as people said they would, as my parents hoped for, as I wanted. At least not at this newspaper, not now. I need time to find words for what I am seeing, for the grief and the killings, for my confusion, for the people who wake up each day and help to keep a hierarchy in place because they are afraid.

The bravest phrase a woman can say is "I don't know." That's my answer when my mother asks what I am going to do with my life if I am leaving the *New York Times*. I don't know.

She gives me a blank face, and some of my friends give me sympathetic looks the way you do when someone is about to file for divorce and you really liked both people in the marriage and you feel sad and wonder what it says about life that two good people couldn't make it work. I don't know.

My last months at the newspaper are a blur of reporting, of long hours and nights out with friends. When a blackout hits that August, the city is flung into a universe without cell phones or computers or subways, and Manhattan turns into a small town. People start walking home. They laugh and curse and eat ice cream at the deli before it melts, and I interview people at the Lincoln Tunnel trying to get rides to New Jersey. An old man hollers, "East Orange! South Orange! Any Orange!"

Maybe it's perfectly acceptable to not know what is going to happen next in life. I walk back to the office in Times Square, where editors are frantically shouting into phones, and I file my story on the oranges. It's after eight or nine when I start the walk home to my illegal studio on the Upper East Side.

Times Square is silent now.

It's not only an absence of sound but also of color. The black billboards loom like empty picture frames. I squint my eyes to adjust to the dark. At Grand Central Station, I can barely make out the grown men in suits stretched out on the sidewalk, their heads on their briefcases, fast asleep, because the trains are not running tonight. The only lights are from the taxis, from the city buses that groan past me, their doors open, people teetering from the steps.

There is comfort in walking through Manhattan when it has been flung into darkness. There is humility, some quietness, and I find that I am not afraid or confused, or maybe it's that when those feelings rise up, I am focused on my feet, on where the sidewalk ends and where the next one begins.

Después

W hen my mother needs to tailor a skirt, to let out the waistband or take it in, she turns the skirt inside out and lays it on the ironing board. She exams the seams, the places where the *hilo* is holding everything together, giving it shape, form, purpose. She adjusts her eyeglasses, makes her decisions, and picks up the scissors, the tiny ones that fit in the palm of her hand. The tips of the blades poke out like extra *dedos*, so that for a moment my mother looks like a woman with seven fingers, two of them silver.

Her hands are swift, almost brutal. She slips the silver *dedos* under the thread and yanks it from its place in the fabric. In English, we would say she's removing the stitching. In Spanish, however, the word is *desbaratar*. If you ask my mother what she's doing with the skirt, she will keep her eyes on the *hilo* and say, "*Desbaratandola.*" Not a taking away, but a taking apart. It is what I am doing here right now, what I have been doing in all the pages before. I have the story, and I am turning it inside out, laying it down on the ironing board, taking it apart with silver *dedos*, *desbaratandola* so I can put it back together again the way I want, the way that makes sense now.

A few weeks after leaving the *Times*, I packed three suitcases. They bulged at the seams with books and a comforter and a map of San Francisco that showed hills and valleys and the bay. Inside each of the three suitcases, I taped a piece of paper with my name and telephone number, in case the bags went missing.

The first time I picked up a copy of *ColorLines* I was in my early twenties. The only magazines I knew were the ones we had subscribed to at the library in my hometown, the kind they sold at Barnes and Noble: *Cosmo, Glamour, Time, Newsweek*. In all those years, I think I only saw a black man on the cover of a magazine once, but it was O. J. Simpson, and *Time* had distorted the color of his face, so I wasn't even sure that counted.

But *ColorLines* had a brown man on its cover, and he was not being accused of murder or of beating his wife, and the story was about the arts fueling social justice. I flipped to the masthead, expecting a Manhattan address, but the magazine was not published in New York. It came from a city I had never heard of, a city that sounded more like a park than a place with sidewalks, electrical poles, parking meters, and people pushing past you. Oakland, California.

My mother was supposed to ride with me to the airport. It was going to be her and me and the three suitcases in the car all the way to JFK, because after the *Times* I was moving to California. But the guy we hired to take us to the airport brought a car too small for my three suitcases and my mother. He said the choice was mine. Either I left a suitcase and took my mother, or I left my mother and took all of my bags.

It must have been around three or four in the morning. Mami and I stood in front of the house on the curb under the branch of a tree. The light post had turned the street silver. My mother's hair, her face, the wrinkles at her eyes, the cars and the shadows, all of it was dipped in silver, and I cried and stared at her for a long time and finally hugged her, because I was taking the three suitcases and leaving my mother.

—∞—

In Oakland, I began working at *ColorLines* and quickly learned that a small magazine is like a big family. There's something to do all the time. There's the toddler who needs to look up for the cover shoot today, the photographer who needs directions, the writer who needs her edits, her proofs, her payment. There's another call to make for the story I'm writing about Gwen Araujo's murder. There are the women after the raid in Postville, Iowa, who need to tell their children's nightmares, their own depressions, their rage, and how the future feels like a page ripped out of a book. There are deadlines and meetings and phone interviews, and a toddler who we hope will look toward the sky.

My mother did not fight with me about California. Neither did my aunties. They are not those kinds of women. Maybe it was because they knew migration. Maybe it was because their own mother had let them leave home. Maybe they thought I was a piece of *hilo* or a word you couldn't keep in your mouth.

After I moved to San Francisco, the city exploded into white dresses.

It was 2004, and women flocked to city hall, holding hands and bouquets, ready to exchange vows and *besos* and white-gold bands with each other. The mayor was marrying them and the male couples who arrived in tuxedos and shiny lace-up shoes.

Over the phone, I pleaded with my mother to visit me. I wanted her to see the sublet studio I was renting in the Mission, the candle for Elegguá I had placed near the front door, and the pink armchair I'd found at the thrift store. My sister though advised me to stop. Mami was seeing enough of *el famoso* San Francisco.

For a few nights, maybe a few weeks, San Francisco pranced across my mother's television screen in Jersey. Telemundo and Univision would have shown the weddings, the promises, *el cariño*.

Even at a distance of three thousand miles, I knew my mother had sighed, as if the news being broadcast were about an earthquake in Colombia. Tía Dora closed her eyes and switched channels. Tía Chuchi shuddered. "I will never travel to Cuba or to California," she told me over the phone. "I hate communists."

I don't know what Tía Rosa did. She is the oldest auntie, and she had spent the nineties pressing her fingers to the television screen whenever Bill Clinton appeared, creating the impression that they were lovers being kept apart by the illogic of miles *y montañas*. She thought he was handsome, and I liked thinking that my oldest auntie understood exiled love, that she nodded in approval when Univision showed women lifting veils and laughing in the new light of their lives.

It is certainly not what she later said about Obama.

"*Ese negro*," she snapped at the flat-screen television in her bedroom, as if the new president of the United States had broken into her Section 8 apartment the night before and tried to steal the dollars she hoarded for the *monjas* in Colombia.

A woman I dated once asked me why I still spoke to my family. It felt like I was running on Mission Street past the botánicas and the bodegas and the Mexican flags and she had stuck her foot out when I rounded a corner. Why do you still talk to them? I stumbled through answers, lurched and teetered and finally fell. I couldn't explain it. But Barack Obama could.

At a podium in Philadelphia in the early months of 2008, he talked about family, about blood family and political family and church family. He declared that he would not banish Reverend Wright from his life. The black pastor was not Obama's father or stepfather. He was not even a tío. And even though the *viejito* believed we had brought September 11 on ourselves, he was family. Obama would not shun him or his grandmother, a white woman who had confessed to him once that when she passed black men on the street, when her pale elbows neared their dark hands, she grew afraid.

I understood what Obama was saying: Some stitches cannot be undone.

After I left, we unraveled, my family and me. I moved to California, *y después*; a year later, my parents sold the house, hired the movers, and migrated to Hialeah, Florida. My sister went to Albany, then DC. My mother's sisters were themselves three long pieces of *hilo*, and they were taken apart over the next ten years. Tía Rosa left for Colombia, promising to die in the house where her mother once fed them boiled eggs. Tía Chuchi moved into her own apartment in New Jersey and filled it with cups of water for the *muertos* and the Virgin Mary. Tía Dora stayed put. She refused to come undone. Even with more trips to the emergency room, she insisted on being *un pedazito de hilo*, her hair a bob of copper around her thin face.

But Thursday came. The doctors had scheduled Tía Dora for abdominal surgery. That was the good part. It meant she was in the hospital. The nurses were nearby, the doctors too. When my tía's heart began to fail, the white coats ran into the room. They had fast hands and they saved my auntie. Afterwards, they transferred her to the cardiac ICU.

The rooms there were in a half circle around the nursing station. One or two patients had visitors. The rest were alone, the tubes strung around their faces like giant bandages. The nurses had swaddled Tía Dora in white blankets, and she was attached to a respirator. Her eyes were wide open, but she was blind. She squeezed my hand. The machines beeped and whirred and flashed their numbers at us.

Us. We were all there. We sat in twos and alone, in separate corners and in silence. Finally, I called us to the bed. "Make a circle," I said, quietly. We did. "Hold hands," I said. We did. After that, I didn't know what to say. My mother paled. Tía Rosa squeezed her prayer book. My sister ate her tears. Tía Chuchi had the rosary beads in her hands, and she began reciting the Hail Mary, and we followed—*Santa María, Madre de Dios, ruega por nosotros*—and we prayed like that for several minutes, giving my auntie over to a mother we hoped was waiting in the sky.

Después, we drove back to Tía Dora's apartment. We tried to sleep, then we called one of her brothers in Colombia. It was dark outside. The kitchen table sat in shadows and so did the bowl of plastic fruit and the glass salt shaker. It must have been five or six in the morning. It must have been later. "*Se nos fue,*" Tía Chuchi wailed into the phone to her brother. *Se nos fue.*

Her brother was confused. He didn't understand. Someone had to say it to him like it was: Tía Dora is dead. She hasn't left us. She's died.

In Florida, my mother tried one factory, and then another. They weren't hiring. They weren't paying. They weren't there. Mami, however, was not a woman to come undone. She registered at the local library for an English as a Second Language class. She sat through lessons about numbers and nouns. She nodded at the teacher and brought cookies for the potlucks. And then, she turned it into business. She did alterations, she told people. She was fast and she didn't charge too much and she was right there in Hialeah, a few blocks from the library.

The women came to her. At first, one or two, then three and four and more. Women in their thirties and forties, their fifties and sixties. Women from Cuba and Colombia and Venezuela and Argentina. Women in fitted jeans and high heels; women with wide blouses and perfumed ears. They were mothers and *abuelas* and wives. They lived down the street, across town, near the hospital.

They didn't leave their homes without lipstick and their hair done and a pocketbook in hand.

The women brought my mother plastic bags filled with their lives, their husband's jeans, their own *faldas*, their teenage daughter's black dress. One woman came with pink pants; another, a bed comforter. They brought my mother their complaints too: the skirt was on sale but it was too long, it was too short, it was impossible to find in life the things you wanted and to the measure that you wanted them.

The women brought news too about car accidents and did you hear about the guy who murdered his girlfriend and three women at Yoyito's on Forty-Ninth? Shot them in the restaurant, right there in the kitchen, then killed himself in his SUV. They shook their heads and murmured prayers and then inspected the seams on the skirt they wanted my mother to take apart.

Sometimes, the women came for my mother but found my father instead. In Florida, in his sixties, my father returned to Cuba. The backyard had a banana tree and a mango tree. My father began wearing sombreros like his uncle and father in Cuba, to keep the sun off his forehead. He planted tomatoes and *calabaza*, and he collected avocados the size of his forearm, and when the women came to pick up their skirts and jeans and comforters, my father pushed bags of produce into their arms. "Take them, take them," he insisted, waving the women away, and so it was. The women carried away their clothes in one bag and giant *aguacates* in the other.

Over and over again, this truth: Writing is how I leave my family and how I take them with me.

Tía Chuchi began writing her memoir.

Her apartment was a second-floor walkup in Jersey. The cups of water gleamed from shelves and night tables and end tables.

The cups of water were for everyone, for Tía Dora and the Virgin Mary and Santa Clara. The cup under her bed, though, did not have kitchen tap water but instead holy water from church, because the *vasito* was meant for her archangel, for his sword and protection and nearness to God.

In that home, surrounded by cups of water, Tía Chuchi began her memoir on a notepad. She drafted an outline first, and when she started writing, she found that one *recuerdo* led to another and that she had to make phone calls to Colombia and inquire about details, because memories are like thread. They can be tugged and loosened and stitched in different directions.

In San Francisco, I looked for the place I came from—the house a city official wanted to condemn when I was a child. I searched for the factories and the booze, the *cuarticos* with African gods and the kitchens where women would be reading cups of water and talking story. I tried to find the mothers and the aunties who might be cleaning offices or hemming a *falda* or correcting some *mocosa*'s Spanish, but the botánica on Mission Street charged too much for a fortune reading and the bodegas sold organic apples and free-trade chocolate. It took me several weeks to realize I wasn't looking for a house or a crooked street or even a familiar face.

The bus was heading south. Mission Street was behind us, and the bus windows were clean enough to see the houses in their floral colors like a chorus of women in house dresses. I was thinking about whether I would find a futon bed at the warehouse whose address I had in my pocket, and how I should not have sold my old futon back in New York, and how hard these lessons are when we first move away from family and we don't know what to take with us and what to leave behind.

We made more stops. The bus grew crowded with brown and black faces and also with plastic bags and tote bags and big purse bags, all those kinds of *bolsas* my mother and my aunties used, because when you don't have a car you have to carry everything with you, and your worst enemy some days is the bus driver, who leaves you three blocks away from the stop you needed.

A woman's voice broke through the crowded aisle. She hollered at the bus driver. Didn't he see that someone had to get off the bus? That someone was trying to get on? That he needed to stop? And I heard what the woman was not saying: That we all wanted to get to where we were going, that the afternoon was long and tired and sun-kissed and everyone here wanted to get home and be kissed in a room they could have all to themselves without their auntie or their mother a few inches away.

The woman's voice made me smile, but then I woke up, as if from a dream. I was about to miss my stop or I already had, and I darted out of my seat and squeezed frantically past shoulders and elbows and plastic bags, the messenger bag bouncing on my back, the address in my pocket. I wasn't going to make it. The front door had already closed, the bus was in motion. The woman, though, she yelled at the driver, and the others joined her, and I felt with a jolt that I was back home. Everyone was trying to help me, but it wasn't about me. It was about us. We all knew what it was like trying to get off the bus.

The bus crawled to a stop then and the door swung open and I flew into the street. I had to walk a little, but it wasn't too far.

Agradecimientos

A mi mami, Alicia Hernández Sosa, por enseñarme el amor sin condicio-nes; a mi papá, Ygnacio Hernández, por apoyarme en mi camino; a María de Jesús Sosa quien además de ser mi tía ha sido mi maestra y mi gran amiga; a Dora Capunay Sosa y José Capunay, quienes respaldaron tanto mi escritura cuando niña; y a Rosa Elena Sosa, por su fe y su fortaleza.

To my sister, Liliana Hernández, who inspires me with her writing and advocacy for foster-care children *y sus familias*, and always knows how to make me laugh.

To Geralen Silberg, my sister-friend, for joining our family with such grace and love.

To Zami, because every writer should thank her cat. Over and over again.

To Erika Martínez and Erica Kremenak, for keeping me on task with love; to Dulce Reyes, for guiding me in the land between Spanish *y el inglés*, and to Bushra Rehman, for *su consejo* to inventory the writing.

To Minal Hajratwala, Sandip Roy, and Peung Vongs, who saw me through the early drafts, and to Catina Bacote, Sunita Dhurandhar, Alberto Ledesma, and Linda González, who gave me feedback and companionship during the revision process.

To David Mura and Maureen Seaton, for reading the manu-script and offering much-needed encouragement.

To Corinne Domingo, who showed up one day with eighty pages of her own writing. I was twenty-one and didn't know that people like me could write books. Thank you.

To Nancy Nordhoff, Amy Wheeler, and the staff at Hedge-brook, for granting me the most divine place to write, read the work of women writers, and make lifelong friends.

To the MacDowell Colony, the Djerassi Resident Arts Program, and Blue Mountain Center, for the generous time and space to draft, revise and be in the company of artists.

To Gary Delgado, Rinku Sen, and the amazing staff at the Applied Research Center and *ColorLines* magazine, for their passion and insights over the years.

To the Center for Fiction in Manhattan, for granting me an affordable office space; to the Barbara Deming Memorial Fund, for my first writer's grant; and to the Rona Jaffe Foundation and Michael Collier, for making my time at the Bread Loaf Writers' Conference possible and nourishing.

To Marcia Ann Gillespie and Gloria Steinem, for inviting me to write for *Ms.* and first find this book. *Mil gracias.*

To Sandra Cisneros, Carla Trujillo, and the Macondo community, for creating a community *con tanto cariño*; to Elmaz Abinader, for the VONA workshops, the VONA *familia*, the VONA love; to M. Evelina Galang and the professors, students, and staff of the MFA program at the University of Miami, who drew me closer to studying craft; and to Angie Cruz, Adelina Anthony, and Marta Lucia, for their collective visions and for the W.I.L.L. (Women in Literature and Letters) workshops in New York where I first found mentors *y comadres*.

To writer-friends *y maestras* who showed me the way: A. Manette Ansay, Anna Alves, Wendy Call, Joy Castro, Carolina De Robertis, Patricia Engel, Lorraine M. López, and Tram Nguyen.

To Jack Alcantara, Pamela Harris, Tracy Kronzak, Tammy Johnson, Leslie LaRose, Keely Savoie, Alice Sowaal, and Susan Starr, for their friendship and *abrazos.*

To my *padrino*, Carlos Aldama, and my *madrina*, Yvette María Aldama, for their brilliance and their music.

To Laura Berenson, Audrey Cleary, Jacob Gershoni, Tereza Iñiguez-Flores, Cary Okano, Sobonfu Somé, Kathie Weston, and the truly precious Engracia, who helped me to trust what I knew.

To the world's best speaker agent, Jodi Solomon, and her staff, for connecting me with countless young people across the country to talk about feminism, racial justice, and the stories we all need to write.

To M. J. Bogatin, for his yes-you-can spirit and professional guidance.

To Gayatri Patnaik, Rachael Marks, and the entire staff at Beacon Press, for bringing this book to you.